The Pain of Helping

BRUNNER-ROUTLEDGE PSYCHOSOCIAL STRESS SERIES
Charles R. Figley, Ph.D., Series Editor

1. *Stress Disorders among Vietnam Veterans*, Edited by Charles R. Figley, Ph.D.
2. *Stress and the Family Vol. 1: Coping with Normative Transitions*, Edited by Hamilton I. McCubbin, Ph.D. and Charles R. Figley, Ph.D.
3. *Stress and the Family Vol. 2: Coping with Catastrophe*, Edited by Charles R. Figley, Ph.D., and Hamilton I. McCubbin, Ph.D.
4. *Trauma and Its Wake: The Study and Treatment of Post-Traumatic Stress Disorder*, Edited by Charles R. Figley, Ph.D.
5. *Post-Traumatic Stress Disorder and the War Veteran Patient*, Edited by William E. Kelly, M.D.
6. *The Crime Victim's Book, Second Edition*, By Morton Bard, Ph.D., and Dawn Sangrey.
7. *Stress and Coping in Time of War: Generalizations from the Israeli Experience*, Edited by Norman A. Milgram, Ph.D.
8. *Trauma and Its Wake Vol. 2: Traumatic Stress Theory, Research, and Intervention*, Edited by Charles R. Figley, Ph.D.
9. *Stress and Addiction*, Edited by Edward Gottheil, M.D., Ph.D., Keith A. Druley, Ph.D., Steven Pashko, Ph.D., and Stephen P. Weinsteinn, Ph.D.
10. *Vietnam: A Casebook*, by Jacob D. Lindy, M.D., in collaboration with Bonnie L. Green, Ph.D., Mary C. Grace, M.Ed., M.S., John A. MacLeod, M.D., and Louis Spitz, M.D.
11. *Post-Traumatic Therapy and Victims of Violence*, Edited by Frank M. Ochberg, M.D.
12. *Mental Health Response to Mass Emergencies: Theory and Practice*, Edited by Mary Lystad, Ph.D.
13. *Treating Stress in Families*, Edited by Charles R. Figley, Ph.D.
14. *Trauma, Transformation, and Healing: An Integrative Approach to Theory, Research, and Post-Traumatic Therapy*, By John P. Wilson, Ph.D.
15. *Systemic Treatment of Incest: A Therapeutic Handbook*, By Terry Trepper, Ph.D., and Mary Jo Barrett, M.S.W.
16. *The Crisis of Competence: Transitional Stress and the Displaced Worker*, Edited by Carl A. Maida, Ph.D., Norma S. Gordon, M.A., and Norman L. Farberow, Ph.D.
17. *Stress Management: An Integrated Approach to Therapy*, by Dorothy H. G. Cotton, Ph.D.
18. *Trauma and the Vietnam War Generation: Report of the Findings from the National Vietnam Veterans Readjustment Study*, By Richard A. Kulka, Ph.D., William E. Schlenger, Ph.D., John A. Fairbank, Ph.D., Richard L. Hough, Ph.D., Kathleen Jordan, Ph.D., Charles R. Marmar, M.D., Daniel S. Weiss, Ph.D., and David A. Grady, Psy.D.
19. *Strangers at Home: Vietnam Veterans Since the War*, Edited by Charles R. Figley, Ph.D., and Seymour Leventman, Ph.D.
20. *The National Vietnam Veterans Readjustment Study: Tables of Findings and Technical Appendices*, By Richard A. Kulka, Ph.D., Kathleen Jordan, Ph.D., Charles R. Marmar, M.D., and Daniel S. Weiss, Ph.D.
21. *Psychological Trauma and the Adult Survivor: Theory, Therapy, and Transformation*, By I. Lisa McCann, Ph.D., and Laurie Anne Pearlman, Ph.D.
22. *Coping with Infant or Fetal Loss: The Couple's Healing Process*, By Kathleen R. Gilbert, Ph.D., and Laura S. Smart, Ph.D.
23. *Compassion Fatigue: Coping with Secondary Traumatic Stress Disorder in Those Who Treat the Traumatized*, Edited by Charles R. Figley, Ph.D.
24. *Treating Compassion Fatigue*, Edited by Charles R. Figley, Ph.D.

Editorial Board

The Pain of Helping

Psychological Injury of Helping Professionals

Patrick J. Morrissette, Ph.D.

Brunner-Routledge
Taylor & Francis Group

NEW YORK AND HOVE

Published in 2004 by
Brunner-Routledge
270 Madison Avenue
New York, NY 10016
www.brunner-routledge.com

Published in Great Britain by
Brunner-Routledge
27 Church Road
Hove, East Sussex
BN3 2FA
www.brunner-routledge.co.uk

Brunner-Routledge is an imprint of the Taylor & Francis Group.
Printed in the United States of America on acid-free paper.

10 9 8 7 6 5 4 3 2 1
Library of Congress Cataloging-in-Publication Data
Morrissette, Patrick J.
   The pain of helping : psychological injury of helping professionals / Patrick J.
Morrissette.
      p. cm. — (Brunner-Routledge psychosocial stress series)
   Includes bibliographical references and index.
   ISBN 0-415-94552-6 (pbk.)
   1. Psychic trauma. 2. Medical personnel—Mental health. 3. Human services per-
sonnel—Mental health. I. Title. II. Series.

RC552.T7M675 2004
616.85'21—dc22
                                    2004001505

To my best friends:
my wife Debbie and beautiful pearls,
Matthew, Alana, and Sam.
Thanks for your continued interest, enthusiasm, and support.

Contents

List Of Tables

Foreword

This important book by Professor Patrick Morrissette of Brandon University in Canada got me thinking about when I first noticed my own "injury" from helping others. It was nearly 30 years ago and I was a young social scientist at Purdue University. Before I tell you about this very useful book, I would like to tell you about this moment of insight for me.

I found myself, once again, driving across the US state of Illinois in 1975. I had made the trip many times. I was engaged in my first postdoctoral research project and studying the immediate and long-term effects of combat exposure from the war in Vietnam. My favorite truck stop along I-70 had the best coffee. My moment of insight was noticing that everyone in view at the truck stop was staring at me. I had just screamed, "aaaaaaaaaaaaaaahhhhhhhhhhh!" It was in response to my dropping the coffee on my foot and the hot coffee spilling over me and the surrounding area. I was late already and this would make me later. When I had gotten on my way I thought about what a fool I had made of myself. A simple accident led to my exploding emotionally. Out of control? Me? You had to be there and to know me to fully appreciate my overreaction. I saw myself then (and now) as a rational, composed, good natured, and (generally) calm person, despite any chaos around me.

"What's going on?" I asked. It dawned on me that I was not looking forward to more interviews. It was not just because I had worked a full week and did not want to lose another weekend. It was not just because setting up the interviews was hard and being late would make it even more difficult. What was going on was that I dreaded absorbing more pain that would surely pour from the souls of the combatants I would interview this day and this weekend. Again.

I then began to recognize how I had changed from this experience. I had become more serious, more focused, angrier and even hostile. I saw it for myself but, more important, those around me — my wife Vickie, my graduate students, my parents, my fellow professors, and even secretaries at Purdue University in my department — noticed how I was different. And they started asking me questions like, "Are you okay?" "What's up?"

Looking back I now recognized that the hundreds and hundreds of interviews and other contacts I was having with the traumatized — especially Vietnam veterans — were traumatizing me. I was the first I knew to develop "compassion fatigue." Long ago I first felt "the pain of help-ing" as a young researcher in the 1970s.

It is, therefore, with great pleasure that I introduce Dr. Patrick Morris-sette's book, *The Pain of Helping*. He explains that he wrote this book first for himself: to first consolidate the extraordinary amount of information available on work-related distress among helping professionals. He wanted to and he succeeded in sorting through all this information to present a brief compendium of useful facts and resources, a kind of clear-ing house on the topic of self care for the busy professional. This is not to suggest that these original sources should be ignored. Indeed, readers will be even more interested in learning more about a particular issue or topic either for themselves, their clients, or their colleagues.

In the process of providing this compendium, Dr. Morrissette offers a useful information synthesis and construct differentiation and does so from the start. Moreover, he helps the reader appreciate the rather com-plicated historical development of traumatology, understand the current status of each construct along with long-standing and current debates, and become familiar with prominent figures in the field.

Beyond the introductory chapter, the book's subsequent chapters focus on the most fundamental constructs introduced in the first chapter (e.g., stress, acute stress disorder, PTSD, compassion fatigue). What is especially useful as a compendium is that each chapter follows a rather consistent, uniform format with the purpose of providing readers with a quick reference to specific areas of interest and with specific practitio-ners.

Professor Morrissette illustrates through this useful book how all of us who work with the traumatized can be affected. More than that he devotes considerable attention to how we know about these effects and trace the conceptual development and sometimes confusion. The final product here is a one-stop resource for all of us and a reminder that what we do is important and that we are not alone in our efforts. I only wish that on discovering my own pain of helping nearly thirty years ago I had a resource like this to guide me.

Charles R. Figley, Ph.D.
Editor, Psychosocial Stress Series

Tallahassee, Florida

Preface

My purpose in writing this book was to consolidate information regarding the various ways that helping professionals could be affected by their work. It was my intent to make this burgeoning information more accessible to practitioners, researchers, educators, and students. This book does not provide a personal explanation of psychological injury or endorse a specific theory. Rather, this book has been designed to summarize existing information and present important references and resources. To avoid superfluous information, I have attempted to present material in a concise manner. I am aware some readers may welcome this direct approach whereas others may find this writing style to be terse.

I will be the first to admit that I was surprised to discover how much topic information was available through a variety of sources. In fact, the flow of information describing how professionals can be affected when experiencing, witnessing, or learning about traumatic events appears endless. There is an ever-growing emphasis on the relationship between human service and helping professional well-being.

Although there are obvious advantages to incoming information regarding helping professional psychological injury, potential confusion and frustration exist due to data overload. Without a central source for information, professionals and students must wade through the literature and explore alternate sources in an attempt to distinguish among the available constructs. It is my hope that this book will spare readers needless frustration and confusion and provide a one-stop source of information.

I understand that new information will emerge as the study of helping professional well-being expands. I also realize not all readers give credence to proposed forms of psychological injury nor do they believe distinctions should be made between constructs. In their opinion, having one or two constructs is ample and adding other constructs is unnecessary.

Readers are encouraged to consider this book as a starting point and a basis upon which future work can be launched. I look forward to productive critique and reading about the different reactions from students, teachers, clinicians, and researchers.

Acknowledgments

I would like to express my sincere gratitude to Emily Epstein Loeb, Associate Editor at Brunner-Routledge, for her unwavering patience, support, and encouragement. I turned to Emily at numerous times for direction and her response was always cheerful and helpful. Emily has a knack for keeping things in perspective and turning challenging tasks into interesting and enjoyable projects.

Introduction

A simple computer search quickly confirms the proliferation of information regarding psychological injury and its far-reaching implications. Significant world and local events such as natural disasters, terrorism, accidents, family violence, and war certainly contribute to the onslaught of information regarding the psychological injury. The systemic repercussions of such tragic events become disturbingly clear for significant others who are vicariously traumatized.

Key Internet search words such as *trauma*, *posttraumatic*, and *stress* produce volumes of data. For some, the vast amount of information can actually appear overwhelming. In the recent past, the familiar constructs of stress, posttraumatic stress, and burnout dominated the literature. As such, locating information and distinguishing among these three constructs was straightforward and the assessment and diagnostic process was relatively easy. During the previous decade, however, a distinct field of inquiry regarding psychological injury has spawned, several new constructs have emerged, and multiple sources of information are now available.

Donovan (1991) has been credited for coining the term *traumatology* (previously referred to as traumatic stress) — a term that has received ample attention (Donovan, 1991, 1993; Schnitt, 1993). According to Donovan, the term *traumatology* was not new to the medical profession and referred to a branch of medicine that dealt with wounds and disability as a result of an injury. Donovan suggested the following definition for traumatology,

> ... the study of natural and man-made trauma (from the "natural" trauma of the accidental and the geophysical to the horrors of human inadvertent or volitional cruelty), the social and psychobiological effects thereof, and the predictive-preventive-interventionist pragmatics which evolve from that study. (p. 434)

When compared to the medical perspective, Donovan contended that traumatology reflected a much broader and overarching field.

THE NEED FOR CONSOLIDATION AND CLARIFICATION

The heightened interest and growth in the area of traumatology underline the need for information synthesis and construct differentiation. Although the development of new constructs has advanced the field of traumatology, the task of locating relevant information and differentiating one construct from another has become more difficult. The study of traumatology now includes contemporary constructs such as secondary traumatic stress (compassion fatigue), vicarious traumatization (VT), critical incident stress, and acute stress disorder (ASD). The growth of traumatology has also been marked by the development of professional journals, books, and organizations. As discussed below, there are consequences to such growth. For example, the introduction and validity of a new construct will be questioned. Also, issues of splintering and information overload emerge.

Construct Refinement and Challenge

Existing information regarding traumatology is being refined and important distinctions are being pursued. As illustrated in the literature, various psychological injury constructs are being deconstructed and put to the test by researchers and practitioners. In concrete terms, the need and validity of each construct is being questioned. For example, Sabin-Farrell and Turpin (2003) provided a critique of vicarious traumatization and asserted: "It is concluded that the evidence to support the existence of VT is meager and inconsistent. Future research needs to be directed at distinguishing VT from other sources of distress arising within the workplace" (p. 449). Robins (1990) focused on posttraumatic stress disorder (PTSD) and wrote, "A valid diagnosis has to be distinguishable from other diagnoses. Because people with PTSD inevitably have symptoms of other disorders, there will remain a question about whether PTSD is itself a distinct disorder" (p. 1676). The validity of acute stress disorder was questioned by Harvey and Bryant (2002) who remarked, "Our review suggests that the theoretical and empirical support for the ASD is flawed and challenges the basis for its continued use" (p. 886). Finally, in reference to critical incident stress, Gist and Woodall (1998, para. 22) charged, "The *critical incident stress* movement was spawned and nourished far outside the critical and conservative waters of scientific psychology, espoused instead through trade magazines, proprietary conferences, and workshops. It can be difficult in such venues to distinguish between rhetoric and research, and faith can sometimes hold more sway than fact."

Construct Splintering

New and valuable information is continually being added to the extant literature (Cardena, 2001). Although this practice can be perceived as needless splintering, differences that exist between constructs have been identified to improve accuracy in assessment and treatment. The fine splintering of constructs (e.g., stress/acute stress disorder and secondary traumatic stress disorder/vicarious traumatization) and the emergence of new names such as traumatic stress (Volpe, 1996), acute trauma (Waters, 2002), acute traumatic stress (Lerner & Shelton, 2001; Pontius, 1993), and severe acute stress (Anshel, 2000) tend to inadvertently complicate matters. In reference to the lack of differentiation among the constructs, Sexton (1999) remarked:

> While there is considerable overlap among these theoretical constructs, there are also differences that have yet to be integrated. This may be because the field of traumatology is still young and as yet there has been only limited research to examine these constructs. (p. 394)

The process of differentiation becomes especially difficult when constructs are loosely or erroneously interchanged, used synonymously, or both throughout the literature (Sabin-Farrell & Turpin, 2003). The inherent problems associated with vague and/or confusing terminology were emphasized by Green (1990). As a result, unique features are ignored and individual constructs are mistakenly perceived as one and the same. Stress and burnout, for example, are often used synonymously and mistakenly interchanged throughout the literature. Efforts to differentiate between constructs, however, should not be overlooked. Donovan (1991), for example, differentiated between trauma and stress and remarked, "Trauma, clearly, is different than stress. While the study of stressors and stress reactions is certainly quite productive, the potential significance of trauma and traumatogenesis and their understanding for the biobehavioral sciences is infinitely greater" (p. 434). When constructs are not properly differentiated, lines of distinction can become blurred and helping professionals can remain uncertain about appropriate assessment, diagnosis, and treatment.

The shared symptoms among constructs demonstrate striking similarities and underscore the challenge of differentiation. Also, construct symptomatology varies depending on the source of information. In acute stress disorder and posttraumatic stress disorder, this problem has been eliminated due to agreed-upon symptomatology appearing in the *Diagnostic and Statistical Manual of Mental Disorders*, (American Psychiatric Association, 2000). Nevertheless, it is only after careful examination that distinctions can be drawn among the remaining constructs.

Information Overload

The influx of new information can contribute to data overload and potential confusion. For some, the rapid growth of traumatology has presented a double-edged sword. On the one hand, there exists a wealth of information that continues to evolve. On the other hand, the extant literature can be very difficult to manage and navigate. The growing number of books and journals devoted to traumatology can appear staggering. Within this literature, however, one begins to see similar information and the absence of *new* news.

BOOK PURPOSE AND ORGANIZATION

The primary intention of this book is to provide readers with a one-stop source wherein prominent psychological injury constructs are clearly defined, consolidated, and accessible. Without a central source for information, professionals are faced with the daunting task of wading through the literature and exploring alternate sources in an attempt to distinguish among the available constructs. An added feature of this book is that readers can become familiar with the historical development of traumatology, understand the current status of each construct along with long-standing and current debates, and become familiar with prominent figures in the field.

This book does not endorse or support a specific construct, theory, or treatment approach. Readers are simply provided with information for their consideration. The amount of information or material that accompanies each construct merely reflects information currently available in an ever-growing field.

Some constructs have benefited from a longer history and increased attention. For example, PTSD appears to have received the greatest attention and boasts a number of diagnostic questionnaires, inventories, books, journals, and organizations devoted to this subject area. According to the Published International Literature on Traumatic Stress (PILOTS, 2003), for example, there are over 22,000 references pertaining to PTSD. Burnout, on the other hand, has not appeared to advance beyond Maslach's pioneering work. The reasons underlying this apparent lack of progress remain unclear.

Toward this end, this book has been organized in a simple and logical fashion. Chapter 1 provides a historical and contemporary view of traumatology and emphasizes the systemic effect of trauma. Moreover, the rippling effect of trauma and its potential impact on intimate partners, family members, significant others, and colleagues is underscored. The various terms that have been used over the years are discussed in their specific context. Perhaps more important, the changing perception of psychological injury as an individual weakness or emotional frailty to a normal human response is highlighted. Chapters 2 through 8 review each of the prominent constructs.

CHAPTER FORMAT

Information regarding each construct has been separated into various sections and subsections. The purpose of this uniform design is to provide readers with a quick reference to specific areas of interest. More specifically, each construct section contains a clinical vignette and subsections devoted to (1) construct overview, (2) symptomatology, (3) affected populations, and (4) intervention. Furthermore, following the summary interested readers will find sections devoted to evaluation resources (structured interviews, diagnostic questionnaires, inventories), and information resources (books, journals, and organizations). Information under affected populations appears in a quick referencing format (e.g., nurses, social workers, emergency personnel). The intervention strategies include those that have been applied to or recommended for helping professionals. Consequently, a number of interventions specific to clients do not appear within this book. It should be noted, however, that similar interventions are used with clients and professionals.

Although only brief descriptions of current articles appear in this book, additional resources (e.g., journal titles, organizational websites) are provided and readers can acquire further information. As noted earlier, some constructs have received more attention than others. In addition, not all constructs are accompanied by well-reviewed assessment information, journals, articles, or organization websites.

CONCESSIONS

From the outset two important concessions must be made. First, despite efforts to draw distinctions among constructs, a degree of information overlap was inevitable due to the common features and shared symptomatology. Perhaps this is the most prevalent argument against the development of new constructs. A critical question might be: *Is a new construct actually different or simply an old wine in a new bottle?* Readers can ponder this question as they read through these pages, track historical and ongoing debates, and formulate their own conclusions.

It is important to realize that of the following constructs, only two appear in the *DSM* (American Psychiatric Association, 2000). These constructs include ASD and PTSD. This does not imply that these two constructs are of greater importance or universally accepted (e.g., Harvey & Bryant, 2002) but rather, that they have been formally recognized by a group of professionals.

On one hand, it can be argued that these two constructs are sufficient and that additional constructs are unnecessary. An opposing argument is that additional constructs have been developed to more accurately describe different forms of psychological injury. A disadvantage of limiting psychological injury assessment to only two constructs is that helping professionals may limit their scope and overlook constructs that may be more appropriate.

Second, by no means is the following information considered exhaustive and, therefore, should be viewed as a preliminary step toward the consolidation and clarification of pertinent information. Obviously, new information is constantly emerging. For example, research findings and information regarding the September 11 tragedy are slowly surfacing. Furthermore, additional information is embedded within related sources that are not cited in this book. Cardena (2001) offered a word to the wise and wrote, "There is a constant increase in formation and development of new instruments, so the researcher/clinician will be well advised to consult regularly with literature databases" (p. 54).

Despite painstaking efforts to provide current and accurate details, important sources of information and treatment approaches may have been inadvertently omitted. It is worth mentioning that although some organizational Web sites were listed, they were not accessible and subsequently excluded. To remain current, the brief annotated descriptions only reflect information that has appeared in recent years. In doing so, of course, many classic works have been excluded. Exceptions were made for constructs that lacked current information and where historical information was needed. Finally, to illustrate available assessment resources, a comprehensive listing has been included. Inclusion of assessment and treatment material should not be perceived as an endorsement by the author.

This book is not intended to replace excellent texts and articles that delve into each construct in much greater detail. It is merely a launching pad from which readers can pursue specific constructs and, perhaps, identify areas that can benefit from future investigation and research. Readers who are interested in obtaining more detailed construct information can refer to the texts, journals, and organizational Web sites that are provided. In conclusion, there are obvious rewards and benefits associated with various helping profession occupations. When describing their work, helping professionals explain how they feel needed, helpful, and appreciated. Maintaining a balance and remembering the positive attributes associated with the helping professions can be challenging when reviewing what can be considered the negative fallout of serving others.

INFORMATION SOURCES

Information contained in this book has come from various sources. A brief description of each source is described below.

National Center for Post-Traumatic Stress Disorder (NCPTSD)

The NCPTSD "was created within the Department of Veterans Affairs in 1989, in response to a congressional mandate to address the needs of veterans with military-related PTSD. Its mission was, and remains: To advance the clinical care and social welfare of America's veterans through research, education, and training in the science, diagnosis, and treatment of PTSD and stress-related disorders. This website is provided as an educational resource concerning PTSD and other enduring consequences of traumatic stress" (National Center for Post-Traumatic Stress Disorder). Publications include the National Center's *Research Quarterlies, Clinical Quarterlies,* a selection of full text articles by National Center staff, and books located in the National Center for PTSD resource center.

Published International Literature on Traumatic Stress (PILOTS)

The PILOTS database is, "an electronic index to the worldwide literature on PTSD and other mental-health consequences of exposure to traumatic events. It is produced by the National Center for PTSD, and is available to the public on computer systems maintained by Dartmouth College. There is no charge for using the database, and no account or password is required. As of 31 August 2002 there were 22,323 references (almost all including abstracts) in the database. The database is updated bimonthly, and a list of the *most recent additions* is available in PDF form" (Published International Literature on Traumatic Stress, 2003).

PsychINFO

PsychINFO, "contains more than 1.8 million citations and summaries of journal articles, book chapters, books, dissertations and technical reports, all in the field of psychology. Journal coverage, which dates back to the 1800s, includes international material selected from more than 1,700 periodicals in over 30 languages. More than 60,000 records are added each year" (Ebsco Publishing, 2003).

The Cumulative Index to Nursing and Allied Health Literature (CINAHL)

CINAHL, "is the Cumulative Index to Nursing & Allied Health Literature, [it] provides indexing and abstracting for over 1,600 current nursing and allied health journals and other publications dating back to 1982 and contains over 700,000 records" (Ebsco Publishing, 2003).

Health Source: Nursing/Academic Edition

Health Source: Nursing/Academic Edition "provides nearly 600 scholarly full text journals, including nearly 450 peer-reviewed journals focusing on many medical disciplines. Also featured are abstracts and indexing for nearly 850 journals" (Ebsco Publishing, 2003).

Sociological Abstracts

The Sociological Abstracts database, "is a primary resource for accessing the latest research sponsored in sociology and related disciplines in the social and behavioral sciences. The database draws information from an international selection of over 1,640 journals and other serial publications, plus conference papers, books, and dissertations" (Ebsco Publishing, 2003)

1

Traumatology: An Overview

The study of human reactions to traumatic events is not new (e.g., Birmes, Hatton, Brunet, & Schmitt, 2003; Weisaeth, 2002). Reports of human reactions to traumatic events, "... can be traced to the earliest medical writings in 1900 B.C. in Egypt" (Figley, 1989a, p. 574). Weisaeth (2002) provided a European history of traumatology and wrote, "The recognition of psychic trauma as a perceived causal factor in psychiatry and psychosomatic medicine and even general medicine has a long pedigree. Homer's *Iliad*, the oldest text in Western literature, is an impressive account of psychological trauma" (p. 443). Specific to posttraumatic stress disorder, Ben-Ezra (2002) suggested evidence of PTSD symptoms extended over the period from 350 years ago to over 4,000 years ago. The historical evolution of PTSD from Freud to the creation of the *Diagnostic and Statistical Manual of Mental Disorders*, fourth edition, (DSM-IV, American Psychiatric Association, 1994) has been discussed by Wilson (1994a).

HISTORICAL PERSPECTIVE

For decades, there has been interest in how people are affected by events outside the normal range of human experiences. Perhaps more than any other area, curiosity surrounding the effect of military and peacekeeping on soldiers has propelled a continued onslaught of research and clinical interest. Weisaeth (2002) wrote,

> A perusal of the scientific history of traumatic stress shows that the Great War, 1914–18, was a watershed. The study of combat stress in that war led to new understanding of traumatic stress disorders, of their etiological and

1

prognostic factors, and of how they could be prevented and treated."
(p. 443)

It appears that interest in the response of soldiers to traumatic and shocking events prompted researchers and helping professionals to eventually consider the effect on others who are exposed to similar experiences. The response to traumatic experiences has received enormous attention and different labels have been created for what is perceived as similar symptomatology.

The following section provides a historical overview and briefly describes how and when various psychological syndromes evolved. More important, such a timeline demonstrates how clinical attention gradually moved from an organic focus to one where individual psychology was recognized. For example, there is a stark contrast between how human responses to trauma were perceived during the U.S. Civil War as compared to the horrific events of September 11. During the Civil War, soldiers who exhibited emotional despair after witnessing human suffering and death were perceived as psychologically defective. The heightened emotional response (e.g., distress, grief, disbelief) of rescue and public service personnel during the horrific events of September 11, however, was viewed as a normal and expected reaction to human devastation. A negative response to caregiver distraught was absent and emotionally wounded caregivers were embraced, comforted, and honored worldwide. Over time, a better understanding regarding the human reaction to trauma has developed and a greater compassion toward the emotional experiences of caregivers has emerged.

Tracing Psychological Trauma Syndromes

War syndromes and evaluation procedures have been tracked. In their historical review, Hyams, Wignall, and Roswell (1996) noted that one of the first studies of a war syndrome was conducted by Da Costa during the U.S. Civil War. Da Costa's paper was published in 1871 and referred to a syndrome described as irritable heart. The symptomatology associated with this syndrome included shortness of breath, palpitations, and sharp or burning chest pain, fatigue, headache, diarrhea, dizziness, and disturbed sleep. During this same period, another war-related illness developed and was referred to as nostalgia. Nostalgia was a severe form of homesickness and the symptomatology of nostalgia included obsessive thoughts of home, extreme apathy, loss of appetite, diarrhea, and sometimes fever.

In his 1920 paper entitled, "Psychology of Effort Syndrome," Culpin mentioned additional syndromes that shared similar symptomatology to irritable heart. These included soldier's heart, effort syndrome, and disordered action of the heart (DAH). Additional terms used to describe these complex symptoms included DaCosta syndrome and neurocirculatory asthenia (Hyams et al., 1996). Soldiers diagnosed with these syndromes presented with fatigue, headache, dizziness, confusion, concentration problems, forgetfulness, and nightmares. Although these syndromes were attributed to physical problems (e.g., heart, nervous weakness, physical weakness, infection), they were also being associated with combat and burial duties.

This finding is important in that a connection was being made between traumatic events and psychological reactions. Moreover, a pure biological etiology was being challenged. Kormos (1978) addressed the organic versus functional polemic and wrote,

> In summary, if there were good reason to assume an organic origin in most cases of combat exhaustion, this would argue against our thesis. However, such is not the case and, furthermore, in situations where some doubt exists, the functional component is generally seen as the more appropriate target of therapeutic intervention. (p. 13)

When reporting on the etiology of effort syndrome, Lewis (1941) wrote, "It is curious and interesting to note that soldiers suffering from heart disease attributed their symptoms to explosion as often as did *effort syndrome* cases; and explosion was also as frequent in aggravating the symptoms in the two groups" (p. 25).

During this period, it appears that the relationship between psychological well-being and impact on physical symptomatology was not rendered serious consideration. Despite reports of terrifying nightmares and battle dreams, there was a tendency to depict soldiers who presented with heart problems as psychologically frail with suspect histories (e.g., childhood nervousness, frights, nocturnal enuresis). This finding supports Figley's (1978) claim: "Prior to the First World War, psychological casualties resulting from war were seen simply as weak, lacking military discipline, or both" (p. xv).

Due to the number of soldiers presenting with effort syndrome, a clinical and research program was established during World War I in the United States and England to determine causes and potential treatment. Initially, symptomatology was attributed to physiological and mechanical factors. For example, the aforementioned symptoms presented by soldiers were considered to be associated with preexisting health problems, cardiac problems stemming from a soldier's clothing and gear (e.g., compression of the thoracic cage), excessive rifle drills, setting-up drills, and so forth (Howell, 1985). Although emphasis was placed on physiological and mechanical factors within this debate, interest in psychological factors gradually emerged. According to Howell (1985), the Irish Surgeon-Major William Riordan, "… advised the army not only to change drill habits but also pay more attention to personal comforts for the recruit in order to make him happier in his new, military surroundings" (p. 36).

Combat stress, otherwise known as acute combat stress reaction, shell shock, or trench neurosis, was also investigated during World War I. Initially, combat stress was attributed to concussions from modern weapons. Eventually, a psychological basis was recognized based on symptomatology that included emotional breakdown during battle, dazed or detached manner, exaggerated startle response, and severe anxiety. This modified position was addressed by Weisaeth (2002) who stated,

> Military authorities could no longer flatly reject that shell shock was a psychological illness, that many brave men succumbed to fear and that neurasthenia could occur in otherwise stable individuals through fatigue and exhaustion. It was no longer acceptable to brand soldiers who broke down because of severe battle stress as dishonorable or to impose punishment on them." (p. 447)

The historical ignorance and intolerance regarding war time psychological disorders has also been addressed,

> It is striking how frequently soldier's heart is discussed by those writing about shell-shock and how infrequently the reverse is true. The explanation may lie in the somewhat lower status accorded to psychological theories of disease than physiological or anatomical heart disease. Perhaps as a result, shell-shock was often equated with malingering or cowardice, and remedy was too often the firing squad. While malingering was often an issue with soldier's heart too, these patients, seem not to have faced capital punishment. (Howell, 1985, p. 43)

Babington (1997) provided a detailed historical account of shell shock and credited Charles S. Meyers, a Royal Army Medical Corps physician, for coining the term in 1915. According to Babington (1997), "… it was a disgrace for a man to go sick with shell-shock" (p. 47). He further elaborated,

> These war neurotics were considered a great nuisance at base hospitals and nobody took much interest in them. As soon as possible they would be transferred to evacuation hospitals, virtually convalescent homes, where they *stagnated* for a while before being sent back to the front. Once they were in action again their neurotic symptoms invariably re-occurred and they had to be returned to base hospitals. (p. 48)

Weisaeth (2002) reported on the convenience of an organic interpretation of shell shock. For example, an organic interpretation saved the self-respect of soldiers and eliminated the need for doctors to diagnose a personal failure or desertion. It is also interesting to note that *granatfieber* (grenade fever) was considered a form of war neurosis. Soldiers presenting with this disorder generally appeared normal except when conditions, especially grenades, at the front were discussed. If grenades were mentioned, these individuals would grow pale, tremble, and sometimes lose control of their legs. Following such an experience they would become restless, nervous, and unable to sleep.

During World War II, effort syndrome received considerable medical attention from the British military. Further, acute combat stress reaction, otherwise known as battle fatigue, combat exhaustion, or operational fatigue, and war neurosis manifested in the form of somatic symptoms and gained greater understanding. As evident during previous conflicts, acute combat stress reaction remained a problem during the Korean War.

An important distinction was drawn between acute combat stress reaction and PTSD during the Vietnam War. It is worth mentioning that PTSD was initially referred to as post-Vietnam syndrome. A distinction between acute combat stress reaction and PTSD pertains to the emergence of symptomatology.

In terms of acute combat stress reaction, there are immediate consequences associated with traumatic events. The consequences of PTSD, on the other hand, are long-term. For example, Vietnam nurse veterans with a diagnosis of PTSD who were exposed to imagery of military-related nursing events showed much higher physiologic responses when compared to non–PTSD nurses (Carson et al., 2000). Based on this study, it appears that witnessing death and injury can result in enduring psychophysiologic arousal.

CONTEMPORARY TRAUMATIC EVENTS

The events of September 11 clearly illustrated the devastating effect of trauma. Eidelson, D'Alessio, and Eidelson (2003) vividly recounted this event and wrote,

> An entire nation was stunned by the destruction of life and property brought on by the crashing of four passenger airliners into the World Trade Center in New York City, the Pentagon in Washington, D.C., and a field outside Shanksville, Pennsylvania. Ultimately, over 3,000 lives were lost

and countless others were forever changed in both obvious and immeasurable ways. The disaster was experienced not only directly by thousands of individuals but repeatedly by millions of television viewers from around the world. For many, the repetitive viewing of the attacks, eyewitness accounts, and stories of survivors and rescue workers had its own traumatizing and retraumatizing effects. (p. 144)

To better understand the psychological impact on caregivers, Eidelson, D'Alessio, and Eidelson (2003) focused specifically on the experience of psychologists. Survey data suggested that psychologists were not immune from the fallout of this traumatic event and reported both positive and negative reactions. Respondents felt good about providing assistance and support to clients and making a genuine contribution to others. They also, however, experienced "... the sense of inadequacy and/or helplessness in the face of such enormity of suffering" (p. 147).

Psychologists struggled with similar issues, feelings of unpreparedness for such magnitude, increased referrals, and increased demands on their time. These professionals had two different responses regarding their personal lives. For example, some felt closer to their families while others experienced feelings of increased anxiety, fatigue, and sorrow over personal loss.

PROGRESSION OF TRAUMATOLOGICAL INQUIRY

Despite its long history, it appears that a closer examination of psychological trauma developed during the past century and has been marked by two distinct phases. The first phase involved challenging the generalization that individuals who demonstrated psychological distress following a traumatic event (e.g., battlefield combat, tragic accidents) were emotionally unstable and susceptible prior to the occurrence of the traumatic event. In reference to rescue workers, for example, Dunning and Silva (1980) stated,

> The prevailing sentiment, both in and out of the profession, is that if you can't take the heat, get out of the kitchen. Such a stance precludes the opportunity for the research and development of screening, training, and support programs to forestall the negative consequences of disaster in those persons who can least afford to be so affected. (p. 289)

It became clear that becoming traumatized after experiencing, witnessing, or learning about a horrific event was a normal human reaction (Waters, 2002) and that the prevalent theory suggesting a predisposition of personal weakness and psychological defect had to be reconsidered and eventually discarded. Until the psychological defect theory was chal-

lenged, traumatized individuals manifesting psychological symptomatology would sometimes be perceived as emotionally unstable and
vulnerable to mental disorders. Their response to a traumatizing event
was evidence of a preexisting emotional fragility. Steed and Bicknell
(2001, para. 1) commented: "Initially, psychological theories, research
and development of effective intervention techniques, methods and processes were client focused." Adherence to these theories disregarded the
influence of an individual's environment and factors that contributed to
an individual's distress were ignored. It appears that due to the absence
of a theory of anxiety, the physical signs of anxiety were misperceived as
symptoms of organic illness (Weisaeth, 2002). Everstine and Everstine
(1993) elaborated,

> The fact is that one's ego must contend with any environmental stimulus
> that comes along. Sudden stimuli must be dealt with swiftly and painful
> stimuli must be met by a healing force. This is true no matter what the per-
> son's *condition* before the event and whether or not the person was emo-
> tionally *vulnerable* in advance. In short, anyone can be traumatized, from
> the most well-adjusted to the most troubled. (p. 7)

Over time, these theories were given less importance and a greater
connection was made between the experience of trauma and normal
human response. On a cautionary note, however, subscribing to a single
theory or broad-brush perspective is discouraged. One should not leap to
conclusions and discount the possibility that some individuals who
appeared psychologically injured following a traumatic event may have
had a preexisting psychological disorder that was aggravated by the
traumatic experience (Regehr, Goldberg, Glancy, & Knott, 2002). As with
most issues, a balanced perspective is encouraged in order to invite varying perspectives and to stimulate debate and discussion.

The second phase, which appeared to take hold during the past
decade, involved an appreciation of how family members and significant others of helping professionals (e.g., mental health workers, emergency medical, fire, and safety personnel, disaster workers) and
caregivers could be vicariously traumatized. The ripple effect inherent
of trauma has been noted and it has been suggested that damage
spreads in waves out from victims to significant others with whom the
victim has intimate contact (Remer & Ferguson, 1998, 1995). Remer and
Ferguson (1998) remarked, "For each primary victim, there are numerous secondary victims — partners, children, parents, family, friends.
When one considers the number of people touched directly or indirectly by the traumatic events, the magnitude of the problem becomes
apparent" (p. 140).

As a result of new insights, the notion of an emotional membrane believed to shield and protect helping professionals and significant others from the emotional effect of a traumatic event was challenged. Appreciating the contagion effect of trauma opened up the new and exciting field of traumatology. As discussed below, the vulnerability and impact of trauma on helping professionals and significant others began to gain increased attention (e.g., Wee & Myers, 2003).

ABSORBING THE PAIN OF OTHERS

Historically, psychological trauma described the emotional experiences of individuals who found themselves in harm's way and minimal concern was devoted to caregivers (Dunning & Silva, 1980; Figley, 1995b; Haley, 1974; Raphael, Singh, Bradbury, & Lambert, 1983).

Attempts, however, have been made to classify types of victims associated with disasters (Shepherd & Hodgkinson, 1990). In 1981, Taylor and Frazer proposed the following victim classification: primary (maximum exposure to a catastrophic event), secondary (grieving relatives and friends), third-level (rescue and recover personnel), fourth-level (community members), fifth-level (individuals affected although directly uninvolved), and sixth-level (survivors who are vicariously affected) (Shepherd & Hodgkinson, 1990).

The importance of secondary trauma has been underscored, "It is highly unlikely that an individual will avoid the direct experience of a traumatic event or events during his or her lifetime. However, if that person is fortunate enough to avoid direct contact with trauma, secondary exposure to the trauma of others is unavoidable" (Williams & Sommer, 1994, p. xiii). Stamm (1997) also presented a literature review that tracked the progressive interest in helping-induced trauma.

The Sin-Eater

A metaphor for people who found themselves psychologically traumatized as a result of their work and service to others was presented by Janik (1995, para. 8). The metaphor is entitled *the sin-eater*. Janik noted that the sin-eater, "... is a social scapegoat role played by members of the superstitious society of Wales during the Dark Ages" and provided the following description,

> In Welsh villages, sin-eaters would eat meals offered by the families of deceased villagers. The food consumed was believed to have absorbed the sins committed by the villager during his or her life on earth, and consumption of the food by the sin-eater released the deceased from obliga-

tory punishment in the next life and freed him or her for heavenly rewards. Sin-eaters ordinarily would consume only a small portion of the food and take the rest home for their families. Thus, sin-eaters and their families were able to survive through their *social service* to the community. (para. 9)

Janik pointed out that earning their sustenance by assuming the role of sin-eater was not inconsequential. For example, realizing that sin-eaters were accumulating the sins of others, villagers would worry about contamination and, thus, view sin-eaters with suspicion. Sin-eaters experienced, "… the honor and degradation of fulfilling a formal social role of scapegoat and detoxifier" (para. 11).

Just as sin-eaters would metaphorically swallow the transgressions and faults of villagers, correction officers harbor toxic and corrosive ideas, images, and memories associated with their work (Janik, 1995). This scenario presents challenges for the individual, significant others, and clients and reminds us that, "There is a cost to caring" (Figley, 1995b, p. 1).

EXPANDING THE PARAMETERS OF TRAUMA

Familiar terms such as *combat fatigue* and *shell shock* characterized the experiences of war veterans. These terms were very useful in helping people better understand the emotional experiences of some veterans. A broader picture eventually emerged and the emotional experiences of other professionals who experienced trauma gained increased attention. Attention was directed to the spillover of traumatic events outside of combat (e.g., emergency personnel). This natural evolution was accompanied by an interest in the vicarious impact of trauma on significant others and caregivers (e.g., offspring, colleagues).

Realizing that personal trauma could extend beyond the actual victim and profoundly effect the lives of significant others, particularly spouses and offspring (Shakespeare-Finch, Smith, & Obst, 2002) exemplified trauma's permeating force. In reference to significant others, "… little, if any direct attention has been paid to identifying them, validating their experiences, or assisting them in either their support of the victims, or even more important, their personal struggles to cope with their own victimization" (Remer & Ferguson, 1995, p. 407). The effect on families was addressed by Nelson and Schwerdtfeger (2002, para. 1) who wrote, "Partners, parents, and siblings often must endure the effects when a family member is traumatized. The family may serve as a resource for support or an obstacle that blocks a traumatized member's recovery." These authors remarked that traumatized parents may be overwhelmed by a personal traumatic experience and can sometimes underestimate their own trauma and how their children are vicariously affected.

There could be a negative impact associated with prolonged service on caregivers and patients (Chen & Hu, 2002). Research conducted by Sisk (2000) supported the notion that "… both caregiving activities and the feelings associated with caregiving may negatively affect the caregiver's ability to participate in various health-promoting behaviors" (p. 41). It has been proposed that caregivers *store away* their emotional pain — a pain which can later devastate individuals, their families, or both (Harbert & Hunsinger, 1991). Realizing that caregivers may hide, underestimate, or otherwise obfuscate their psychological distress is a disconcerting scenario that warrants ongoing attention.

Helpers and Family Traumatization

A more complete consideration regarding the systemic costs of caring within families was offered by Figley (1998); the researcher asserted that the field of traumatology has overlooked families and other supporters of psychologically injured people. As described below, families could be traumatized via simultaneous effects, vicarious effects, chiasmal effects, and intrafamilial trauma (Figley, 1989a).

Simultaneous Effects

The simultaneous effect refers to when an entire family experiences a traumatic event. In general families who are traumatized, "… are relatively free of disaster-related emotional difficulties" (Figley, 1989a, p. 19). According to Figley this response could be attributed to the fact that the event is shared by a group whose members can provide mutual support.

Vicarious Effects

It was Figley's (1989a) contention that individuals could be vicariously traumatized when learning about events experienced by significant others. For example, a father can experience emotional trauma when learning about a catastrophe involving his son or daughter. Figley suggested that a significant other may experience more stress than an actual victim.

Chiasmal Effects

Originally termed *secondary catastrophic stress response*, chiasmal effect refers to a process whereby significant others are emotionally touched when attending to the victimization of a close friend, relative, or family member. Significant others are affected through their efforts to help. Referring to an earlier study regarding crime victims and their supporters, Figley (1989a) wrote,

> ... as expected, the major predictor of *supporter distress was victim distress* [and] it is clear that a pattern of effects emerged in both the victim and supporter. The crime victims as well as their supporters suffered from the crime episode long after the initial crisis had passed. (p. 20)

Intrafamilial Trauma

Figley (1989a) stated: "Families certainly have the capacity to be extremely helpful in enabling family members in recovering from traumatic stressors. They may become traumatized through their assistance" (p. 21). It is only logical that the close bond between family members would increase a likelihood of shared trauma.

Family Burnout

In an attempt to better understand how families can be affected by trauma, for example, Figley (cited in Peeples, 2000) described *burnout* in families. Based on earlier interviews regarding combat-related stress disorder, Figley discovered that family members "... were living the war indirectly through the emotional responses of their veteran family member" (Peeples, 2000, para. 2).

As the construct of secondary trauma was emerging, caution was recommended regarding global and unsubstantiated statements (Jenkins & Baird, 2002; Waysman, Mikulincer, Solomon, & Weisenberg, 1993). It was noted:

> There is a growing body of literature on secondary traumatization, but it is almost entirely anecdotal. There have been virtually no systematic empirical studies aimed at documenting and understanding these phenomena. Very little is thus known about factors that may influence the process of secondary traumatization, such as the degree of empathy and responsibility family members feel for one another, the quality of the marital relationship, the social climate, and so forth. (Waysman et al., 1993, p. 104)

As discussed below, the void regarding secondary trauma research was acknowledged and is gradually being addressed.

HELPING PROFESSIONAL TRAUMA RESEARCH: ANSWERING THE CALL

Over the years, researchers have begun to answer the call for more investigation regarding caregiver burden and strain (Sisk, 2000; Chen & Hu, 2002) and secondary traumatization (e.g., Baird & Jenkins, 2003; Bride, Robinson, Yegidis, & Figley, 2003; Dunning & Silva, 1980; Raphael, Singh, Bradbury, & Lambert, 1983). Preliminary research also demonstrates a relationship between the degree of exposure to trauma-associated material and the experience of secondary traumatic stress disorder (Arvay & Uhlemann, 1996; Collins & Long, 2003; Follette, Poluusny, & Milbeck, 1994; Kassam-Adams, 1995; Motta, Kefer, Hertz, & Hafeez, 1999; Nelson-Gardell & Harris, 2003; Ortlepp & Friedman, 2002; Pearlman and Maclan, 1995; Raingruber & Kent, 2003; Schauben & Frazier, 1995; Steed & Bicknell, 2001; Wee & Meyers, 2003). Specific programs to assist helping professionals have also been designed (Gal, 1998; Klingman, 2002). Although ongoing research is necessary to better understand the relationship between helping professional vulnerability and secondary traumatization, important inroads have been made.

TRAUMATOLOGY AND PSYCHOLOGICAL INJURY CONSTRUCT DEVELOPMENT

As evidenced by the proliferation of books, journals, and organizations, the field of traumatology has received enormous attention and has experienced tremendous growth in the past decade (Donovan, 1991, 1993; Green, 1990, Schnitt, 1993). According to Figley (1995a), "Traumatology, the study of traumatic stress, has literally been invented in the last decade" (p. 573). While providing a historical overview of posttraumatic stress disorder, Wilson (1994a) reflected on major world events of the 20th century and remarked,

> When it is considered that hundreds of millions of human lives have been adversely affected by such traumatic events, it only stands to reason that sooner or later scientific inquiry would accumulate enough momentum to begin examining the multifaceted aspects of what traumatization means and then potential long-term impact to human lives of such events. (p. 682)

There are a number of constructs describing the deleterious effects of trauma on helping professionals who have experienced, witnessed, or learned about shocking events within the field of traumatology. The

more popular constructs include PTSD, secondary traumatic stress disorder (compassion fatigue), ASD, stress, burnout, VT, and critical incident
stress. The increase in construct development might be influenced by the
willingness of helping professionals to discuss the emotional fallout of
their work. For example, Cornille and Woodward Meyers (1999, para. 7)
discussed the secondary traumatic stress among child protective service
workers and remarked:

> Studies concerning secondary exposure to traumatic material have focused
> primarily on the traumatization of crisis workers (i.e., paramedics, firefight-
> ers, emergency medical technicians, police officers, rescue workers, disaster
> response teams) and psychotherapists. CPS workers, however, are just as
> likely as crisis workers and psychotherapists to be directly exposed to a
> number of children's traumas and personal traumas on a daily basis
> throughout their careers.

In regard to the medical profession, Pfifferling and Gilley (2000, para.
5) wrote, "The medical profession, with its tremendous physical and
emotional demands, naturally predisposes physicians to compassion
fatigue." "In the past, the connection that many family physicians shared
with their patients gave them the replenishment they needed to cope
with the stressors of practicing medicine. But today, increasing demands
have caused some physicians to stop taking the time to appreciate the
love, respect, and appreciation that their patients want to share with
them."

The secondary traumatic stress within the nursing profession was
explored by Martin (cited in Joinson, 1992) who wrote, "Because your
profession sets you up for compassion fatigue, you'll almost certainly
experience it at some point in your career" (p. 119). In her examination of
nurse stress, Larson (1987) listed several themes (e.g., feelings of
inadequacy, emotional overinvolvement, excessive demands, desire to
quit the profession) that apparently contributed to stress experienced by
nurses.

Concerns regarding the emotional welfare of healing professionals
have been echoed by others. Milstein, Gerstenberger, and Barton (2002),
for example, believed that healing professionals who work with seriously
ill patients may be particularly vulnerable to stress symptoms. They pre-
dicted a grim outlook for psychologically injured professionals, "Left
unattended these professionals may go down the dark road leading to
burnout, with impaired effectiveness as caregivers, diseases rooted in
stress, as well as increased suicides, drug and alcohol addiction, and
exacerbation of personality disorders" (p. 917).

It has been pointed out that, "Until recently, it was thought that trauma workers, because of their special training, were immune to traumatic stress and reactions" (Cornille & Woodward Meyers,1999, para. 3). Feinberg (2002) discussed the systemic impact on school personnel who supported children and families during the terrorist attacks of September 11 and asserted that school personnel played a pivotal role in the healing process and were thrust into the role of crisis caregivers. He further wondered, "But while the schools are providing the support needed by children and families in overcoming the trauma of September 11, who is providing the same type of support for the schools' caregivers?" (p. 9).

IMPORTANCE OF HELPING PROFESSIONAL WELL- BEING

The importance of professional emotional well-being is critical when considering the role of these professionals as parents, intimate partners, and caregivers. In discussing the prevention of secondary traumatic stress (STS), Yassen (1995) asserted, "... unless we prepare, plan, or attend to the effects of STS, we can cause harm to ourselves, those who are close to us, and to those who are in our professional care" (p. 179). Morrissette (2001) described the process of self-supervision and the ways in which helping professionals could monitor their own well-being.

Shared Trauma

Saakvitne (2002) broached the issue of shared trauma between therapists and clients and underlined therapist vulnerability. She reported that many clinicians are experiencing multiple levels of traumatization and believed a shared tragedy can alter one's work habits. For example, a professional and client might become increasingly aware of the professional's vulnerability. When this occurs, professionals might feel deskilled, guilty, or ashamed. Saakvitne (2002) went on to ask, "How does that personal awareness change our availability, our ability to track the patient's affects, our vulnerability to responding in concordant or complementary ways to transference?" (p. 444).

In underscoring the systemic impact of trauma, traumatologists have acknowledged the vicarious effect of domestic violence, disasters, murder, and terrorism. Consequently, the definition of *victim* has been expanded and reaches beyond those who are directly affected by a traumatic event. The increased number of citizens who are exposed to single or multiple incidents of trauma through automobile or industrial accidents, civil disorders, kidnapping, and other violent crimes has long been acknowledged (DeFazio, 1978).

Effects of Vicarious Trauma

In describing an interactional theory of traumatic stress, Wilson (1994b) likened the level of social, economic, and personal support present as the trauma membrane. In this process, significant others tend to form a protective membrane of support around the victim. The secondary stress that can result from participating as part of such a membrane is a concern for victims and significant others. Advantages and disadvantages are associated with learning about traumatic events. Advantages include feeling helpful, an increased level of intimacy or connection, and a greater sense of identity. Disadvantages include feeling overwhelmed and emotionally paralyzed. The distress experienced by significant others usually pertains to the vicarious trauma coupled with their perceived inability to immediately alleviate the pain of the victim. In reference to the latter issue, counselors report shutting down emotionally during the disclosure and dialogue process. When explored, this reaction is not propelled by an inherent disinterest but, rather, an automatic self-protective mechanism that serves to guard against further discomfort. This response is similar to what Scott and Stradling (1994) referred to as cognitive avoidance. During this stage, significant others avoid thinking about the traumatic event(s) or aspects of it.

Not knowing how to respond to the individual who is describing an event further exacerbates the situation, leaving significant others feeling confused, incompetent, and distraught. Although genuinely interested in alleviating the distress of victims, they are uncertain how to do so. The feeling of disempowerment can be prompted by stories that evoke concerns about their own personal power or efficacy in the world (McCann & Pearlman, 1990). Ensuing responses can vary and may include efforts to increase personal safety, heightened awareness regarding the unpredictability of life, increased need for freedom and personal autonomy, and so forth.

As victims vividly describe traumatic events, significant others become both witnesses and participants in traumatic reenactments (Pearlman & Saakvitne, 1995). Consequently, they are faced with the challenge of remaining emotionally present and empathic while attempting to ward off vexatious reactions. Herman (1992) suggested that in attempting to gain an understanding of psychological trauma, one comes face to face with human vulnerability and capacity for evil in human nature. As such, "... when the traumatic events are of human design, those who bear witness are caught in the conflict between victim and perpetrator (Herman, 1992, p. 7).

Although not all significant others who are privy to stories of trauma experience psychological distress, the potential influence of a story cannot be underestimated. As stated earlier, the vicarious trauma experienced by an individual can extend beyond oneself and have ramifications for immediate family, friends, colleagues, and so forth. Individuals who are vicariously traumatized may experience a sense of disorientation, terror, and vulnerability. Not realizing the extent to which they have been influenced as a result of listening to a painful narrative, the significant other may initially have difficulty accounting for mood and behavioral vacillations. Because the described event did not directly involve them, many individuals struggle to associate their emotional disposition with the narrative that unfolded in front of them.

ETHNICITY AND TRAUMATIC STRESS

Interest in the area of ethnicity within the field of traumatology remains modest. In fact, very little attention has been devoted to this subject area. Parson (1985) underscored the important relationship between ethnicity and trauma response and asserted,

> Ethnicity also shapes how the client views his or her symptoms, and the degree of hopefulness or pessimism toward recovery. Ethnic identification, additionally, determines the patient's attitudes about sharing troublesome emotional problems with therapists, attitudes toward his or her pain, expectations of the treatment, and what the client perceives as the best method of addressing the presenting difficulties. (p. 315)

Parson (1985) encouraged helping professionals to broaden their view, appreciate different cultural idiosyncrasies, and avoid a blanket perspective regarding trauma response. Toward this end, Morrissette and Naden (1998) presented an interactional view of traumatic stress within the Aboriginal and First Nations context.

Aboriginal and First Nations Counseling and Traumatic Stress

Aboriginal and First Nations (AFN) counselors frequently report emotional turmoil while attempting to identify the source of their despair following a client disclosure of trauma. Although not having been directly affected by the traumatic events being described, they are, nonetheless, left grappling with their own emotional, spiritual, and physical reactions. Remer and Ferguson (1995) remarked,

For some period of time, while accommodation, shock, denial, and confusion occur, the secondary victim will experience being off balance and out of touch. Length and degree of disorientation will depend on a number of factors—environmental, intrapsychic, and interpersonal—many of which will be directly related to pretrauma experiences. (p. 410)

Morrissette and Naden (1998) elaborated on an interactional view of traumatic stress among AFN counselors and underscored the extraordinary bond and respect for extended family within the traditional Native culture. This closeness presents a unique complexity into the disclosure process among First Nations peoples. An individual's despair and grief can also extend throughout the First Nations community. The strong sense of family and mutual responsibility tends to collapse the emotional proximity within the First Nations culture. This unique cultural emotional characteristic is significant in that the degree of distress experienced by caregivers is not necessarily greater within immediate family relationships. As noted by Wilson (1994b), "When trauma affects an entire community, it can produce many secondary stressor experiences if the destruction or devastation is severe enough" (p. 10). A serious implication of this cultural characteristic pertains to the fragmenting effect trauma can have on a community. Overcome by a personal sense of shame and humiliation, trauma victims begin to isolate themselves and withdraw, thus breaking the natural social bond and hindering the healing potential within the community. As such, an overall result of such fragmentation is the elimination of many sociocultural support systems necessary for recovery (Wilson, 1994b). Within the First Nations community, for example, victims may avoid participating in spiritual healing rituals and limit contact with others. Being nonintrusive by nature, significant others avoid infringing on personal space by remaining respectful of interpersonal boundaries and personal choice. Therefore, in many cases, victims tend to fragment away from the larger community and their own families. As the traumatized counselors withdraw and isolate themselves, intimate and family relationships can be disrupted. For example, it is not uncommon for an intimate partner of the traumatized counselor to assume that a relationship problem exists when his or her partner becomes increasingly distant and exhibits mood fluctuations. Children as well can be affected when a traumatized parent is less available and preoccupied with his or her own personal distress. As the traumatized parent becomes incapacitated, child-rearing responsibilities can be shifted to the alternate parent. Feeling overburdened with parental duties, the alternate parent pursues his or her partner for assistance. In response, the traumatized parent continues to withdraw, thus fueling a vicious cycle and exacerbating the situation.

TRAUMA HISTORIES OF HELPING PROFESSIONALS: DOES IT MATTER?

Yassen (1993, para. 1) observed, "It is not uncommon for clinicians treating survivors of traumatic events to have a personal history of traumatization." The question of whether a helping professional's traumatic history influences his or her work, emotional disposition, or both, however, remains questionable. Based on existing research, results are mixed and inconclusive. Despite the lack of empirical evidence, however, *soft spots* and *vulnerabilities* are considered underlining concerns for counselors with a history of trauma (Horwitz, 1998; Miller, Britton, Wagner, & Gridley, 1998). Miller and colleagues (1998) remarked that counselors with a long history of unresolved sexual abuse and related problems (e.g., employment, relationship) possess soft spots. According to these authors, soft spots can be reopened by critical events resulting in the rewounding of counselors. "A traumatic childhood may allow greater identification with the client and an opportunity to repair or master old wounds. This *wounded healer* notion has been previously referenced and can be traced to the time of ancient Greeks" (O'Connor, 2001, p. 346). Figley (1995a) appeared more convinced and asserted that "... unresolved trauma in the therapist's life will be activated by reports of similar trauma in clients" (p. 575).

Qualitative and quantitative research orientations have been used to explore this controversial area. The countertransference experiences of psychotherapists with histories of psychiatric hospitalization were explored through interviews and it was concluded that "... wounded healers experience a range of countertransference issues, including varying degrees of identification with clients" (Cain, 2000, para. 1). Participants reported both positive and negative impacts of countertransference.

After interviewing trauma psychotherapists, Benatar (2000) determined there was no significant difference in the area of vicarious trauma between professionals with a sexual abuse history and those who reported no such history. She further asserted, "The results of this study do *not* support the caveats in the literature concerning the special vulnerability of therapists with a CSA history" (p. 23).

A personal history of childhood abuse and the heightened risk of secondary traumatic stress in child welfare workers have invited interest. For example, results indicated that "... personal experience of childhood trauma in the form of child abuse and neglect increases a child welfare worker's risk of STS" (Nelson-Gardell & Harris, 2003, p. 21). According to this study, emotional abuse or neglect appeared to be issues that placed workers most at risk. Similarly, Ghahramanlou and Brodbeck (2000) found that a positive personal trauma history was helpful in predicting secondary trauma among counselors who work with sexual assault victims

Follette, Poluusny, and Milbeck (1994) surveyed mental health and law enforcement professionals and assessed current and past trauma experiences, exposure to client traumatic experiences, and the consequences of these experiences when serving child sexual abuse victims. In terms of mental health professionals, those who reported a history of childhood physical or sexual abuse did not differ significantly on several variables from those who did not have a history of abuse. In fact, helping professionals who reported personal childhood abuse events used more positive coping behaviors when dealing with sexual abuse cases.

Law enforcement professionals who reported a history of childhood abuse revealed a greater use of negative and positive coping strategies when compared to nonabused law enforcement professionals. However, no significant differences in the number of negative responses to investigating sexual abuse cases were found between abused and non-abused officers. In summary, Follette and colleagues (1994) reported:

> Mental health professionals reported relatively low levels of general psychological distress, trauma symptoms, and PTSD symptoms despite reporting moderate levels of personal stress. Law enforcement professionals, however, were significantly more distressed than mental health professionals on all measures of psychological symptoms. (p. 219)

The prevalence of childhood trauma, family dysfunction, and the psychological distress among female mental health professional and women working in other professions has also received attention (Elliott & Guy, 1993). Results from this study showed that women who worked in the mental health field were more frequently traumatized during childhood than were women who worked in other professions. It also appeared that female mental health professionals came from more chaotic families of origin. Despite these results, however, it was concluded that female mental health professionals "... experience no greater and in many areas significantly less, psychological distress than do other professionals" (p. 89).

A study conducted by Pope and Feldman-Summers (1992) surveyed clinical and counseling psychologists. These authors were interested in determining (a) the proportion of psychologists who reported having been sexually or physically abused; (b) how these professionals assessed the quality of their training in the area of abuse; (c) whether these professionals believed that they were competent to help clients who were reporting abuse; and finally (d) the interrelationship of gender, professional degree, history of abuse, perceived adequacy of training, and perceived competence. The results from this study indicated a relatively high number of study participants had experienced physical or sexual abuse, participants considered their graduate training and internships in the area of abuse deficient, and participants considered themselves moderately competent to help abuse victims; and, when compared to their male counterparts, female practitioners reported a higher level of perceived competence.

Briere (1992) considered the effects of childhood abuse on helping professionals and discussed the concepts of overidentification, projection, boundary confusion, and abuse-related countertransference. In providing a balanced view he addressed both advantages and disadvantages of an abuse history.

SUMMARY

Interest in how people react to traumatic events has a long and fascinating history. This chapter briefly tracked the evolution of traumatology during different world events. The purpose in doing so was to illustrate how society has changed toward those who are in harm's way. During this evolutionary process, there was a shift in perspective whereby individuals presenting as psychologically injured were no longer viewed as psychologically deficient but, rather, reacting normally to events outside the range of normal experiences.

Over the years, the field of traumatology has blossomed and has developed through distinct stages. The first stage involved normalizing the reactions of helping professionals who experienced, witnessed, or learned about horrific tragedies. The second stage involved appreciating and understanding how helping professionals could absorb the emotional pain of those they are helping. Finally, the impact of the helping professional's work on family members, significant others, and colleagues of helping professionals was realized.

The growing interest in the traumatization of helping professionals has also been accompanied by the development of additional constructs and gradual research. There are, however, scholars who remain skeptical about the need for additional constructs and the quality of available research. These scholars ask important questions and play a critical role in better understanding how helping professionals are affected by their work.

As one would expect, having a history of abuse does not necessarily mean professional helpers would be at an advantage or disadvantage. According to the literature, the degree to which a history of abuse affects helping professionals is a complex matter and is dependent upon the individual. A review of the literature supports the need for ongoing research in the areas of trauma and ethnicity and the influence of personal trauma histories among helping professionals.

2

Stress

Sherry was a mature and competent professional who entered the psychiatric nursing profession with enthusiasm and career aspirations. On her drive to work, Sherry reminisced about her academic training and the thrill of her first job. With seniority and increased responsibilities, however, Sherry's view of work and life began to gradually change.

Although once enjoying the unpredictable nature of her job, Sherry became fearful and increasingly anxious. She resented aspects of her work and particularly disdained what appeared to be an endless onslaught of needless paperwork. The jovial attitude that Sherry was well known for was replaced with frustration and irritability. She found it difficult to socialize with colleagues and felt lonely on the job.

During her first few years as a nurse, Sherry enjoyed the adrenaline rush when distressed patients would call for immediate support. Sherry prided herself on effective intervention and case management. Events that once seemed exciting, however, began to contribute to Sherry's anxiety and worry. She found herself lying awake at night thinking about patients and her mounting responsibilities. It wasn't usual for Sherry to experience rapid thinking and a pounding heartbeat as she obsessed about her work and various scenarios. Frustrated with the inability to sleep, she would rise early feeling emotionally drained and lethargic.

The morning conversations she and her husband typically enjoyed over breakfast were interrupted and eventually replaced by Sherry's concern about clinical documentation and the need to organize her day. Sherry would often forget arrangements she had made with her husband and resented any added pressure. As Sherry's attitude and behavior deteriorated, she followed her supervisor's advice and agreed to seek the assistance of an Employee Assistant Program counselor to discuss her elevated stress and growing sense of disorganization and unhappiness.

CONSTRUCT OVERVIEW

Stress has received enormous attention and has been defined in a number of ways throughout the literature (Goldenberg & Breznitz, 1993). In providing a working definition, Stoyva and Carlson (1993) suggested psychological stress "... refers to a situation in which the challenges or threats facing the individual exceeds his or her estimated coping mechanisms (p. 729). According to Pines (1993), "Stress happens to more people and in more situations than burnout" (p. 386). It was her contention stress did not cause burnout and people are able to excel in stressful situations if they feel their work is meaningful. Specific symptoms indicating stress have been outlined by Goldenberg and Breznitz (1993).

AFFECTED POPULATIONS

As demonstrated below, stress has been reported within various helping professions and also within specialty areas (e.g., counselors working specifically with HIV/AIDS clients, mental health nursing).

Counselor Stress

O'Halloran and Linton (2000) noted, "The challenge lies in the fact that wellness is a concept that we as counselors often focus on more readily for our clients than ourselves. Counselors who are trained to care for others often overlook the need for personal self-care and do not apply to themselves the techniques prescribed for their clients" (p. 354). These authors provided a list of resources while addressing counselor stress.

Earlier research conducted by Sowa and May (1994) considered occupational stress within the counseling profession with an eye on training. Results from this study concluded that occupational stress wasn't necessarily inherent in the counseling profession. Moreover, the interaction between professionals and their counseling environment appeared to be a critical feature in determining the level of counselor stress.

HIV/AIDS Counseling. There is a possibility that counselors could journey into the unknown when working with an HIV/AIDS client population (Kiemle, 1994). The issues of death and dying, disease, disability, and disfigurement can be extremely disturbing for counselors. Moreover, a counselor's ability to contain and cope with such sensitive issues can be challenging and possibly lead to burnout unless addressed in supervision.

TABLE 2.1
Stress Symptomatology

Emotional	Cognitive	Physical	Behavioral
Despair	Inaccurate and negative appraisals of self	Headaches	Impatient
Guilt	Dissociative amnesia	Back pain	Increased dependency
Depressed		Heart palpitations	Frequent crying spells
Emotional numbing	Thoughts of impending death	Rapid, pounding heartbeat	Blaming
Overexcitability	Pessimistic	Tightness of chest	Nail biting
Anxiety	Confused	Sleep problems	Overeating
Fearful	Rapid thought process	Hyperventilation	Loss of appetite
Excessive worry	Distrustful	General weakness	Grind/clench teeth
Feeling trapped	Forgetful	Tremors	Poor interpersonal relationships
Isolated	Obsessive thinking	Dizziness	Nervous laugh
Lonely	Worry	Dry mouth	Lethargic
Loss of Control		Increased perspiration	Accident prone
Embarrassed		Nausea	
Unhappy		Fatigue	
Discouraged		Tense neck and jaw	
Irritability		Nightmares	
Bad Temper		Throat constriction	
Frustrated		Difficulty swallowing	
Helpless		Muscle cramps	
Hopeless		Ulcers	
Flattened affect		High blood pressure	
Resentful		Colon problem	
Sad		Shaky/stuttering voice	
Lack a sense of humor		Trembling/shaking Gas pains/ constipation Acid stomach/ heartburn Sexual difficulties Diarrhea	

Note: Adapted from http://www.stresstips.com.

Nurse Stress

Mental Health Nursing. Stating that mental health nursing could be a stressful enterprise, Sharkey and Sharples (2003) made an effort to investigate and mitigate stress experienced by these professionals. Toward this end, through research they developed a learning pack aimed to "... encourage and develop collaborative working practice" (p. 73). Based on their results, these authors discovered that their learning pack led to a reduction in work-related stress.

It has been suggested that mental health nurses experience high levels of stress (Edwards, Burnard, Coyle, Fothergill, & Hannigan, 2000). Organizational pressures and factors related to patient care were considered to be significant contributing factors to nurse stress. For example, study participants reported that long waiting lists, poor resources, and constant interruptions contributed to their stress.

Mental health nursing is a potential emotional minefield with different types of stressors when compared to the general nursing population (Kipping, 2000). Mental health nurses work with patients who can be dangerous, unpredictable, or incapable of communication. Kipping also addressed the potential fallout from stress in mental health nursing and included elevated compensation settlement claims, nurse attrition, the lack of continuity of care, and eventual burnout.

Psychiatric Nursing. Seven distinct areas of stress among psychiatric nurses have been identified (Leary, Gallagher, Carson, Fagin, Bartlett, & Brown, 1995). Based on a small sample of nurses who participated in brief interviews, it was determined stress was embedded in the following areas: professional isolation, lack of support, unrealistic organizational expectations, organizational pressure, lack of time for professional development, ineffective communication, and working with difficult patients.

Correctional Nursing. Seventeen thousand of the 2.2 million employed registered nurses in 2000 worked in correctional nursing (Flanagan & Flanagan, 2002). Reportedly, correctional nursing was a specialty growing in size and complexity. To further investigate job satisfaction and job stress among correctional nurses, these authors conducted a study aimed at identifying factors that contributed to job stress among these professionals. Several factors were identified (e.g., a perceived lack of understanding and support from organizational superiors, time pressure, and fluctuations in workload).

Forensic Nursing. Attention, albeit limited, has been devoted to stress among nurses who practice forensic mental health (Coffey & Coleman, 2001; Coffey, 1999; Happell, Pinikahana, & Martin, 2003). In their study, Coffey and Coleman (2001) found a significant association between caseload size and level of stress. Other important information discovered by these researchers was that managerial and collegial support was important in ameliorating stress. In reference to caseload, they reported:

> Factors that may be important to nurses in terms of caseload include mix of patients and the perception of a constantly increasing caseload. For instance, managing potentially violent situations in the community or cop-

ing with a self-harming client and the fear of being held personally responsible for such incidents are important. (p. 403)

Based on a survey of forensic psychiatric nurses, it was discovered that participants did not experience high levels of stress (Happell et al., 2003). Not surprisingly, however, participants did report heightened stress when there was insufficient time to support patients, complete tasks, or cover the unit.

Community-Based Nursing. As a result of change and uncertainty within community nursing, it has been argued that stress within community nursing has been overlooked (Evans, 2002). It has been further emphasized that expectations are placed on nurses to contribute with less time, money, and equipment.

Evans summarized her research findings into six themes including: imbalance between amount of work and staff (understaffing), no time to adjust to change, lack of managerial support, interagency relationships, some aspects of direct patient care, and family and work responsibilities.

Stress and mood disturbance among nurses has been explored (Healy & McKay, 2000). Results from this study suggested workload was the highest perceived stressor among nurses. Interestingly, conflict with other nurses and a lack of staff support were the least reported stressors.

Rodney (2000) studied the relationship between aggressive behavior exhibited by patients with dementia and nurse stress. It was suggested that behavioral problems presented by patients with dementia can distress caregivers and that threatening patient behavior was correlated with high stress. Additional questions that emerged from this research were: Do younger or less experienced nurses perceive higher levels of threat? Do nurses who have been previously injured by patient's experience increased threat appraisal?

Hospital-Based Nursing. A survey of Hong Kong nurses indicated that major sources of stress were related to work overload, interpersonal relationships, and interactions with hospital administration (Callaghan, Tak-Ying, & Wyatt, 2000). Similar findings and concerns were expressed by oncology unit nursing staff (Escot, Artero, Gandubert, Boulenger, & Ritchie, 2001). Healy and McKay (1999) found that workload was perceived as the most frequently occurring source of stress in their study of nurses in Victoria, Australia.

In a Canadian study, Tyson, Pongruengphant, and Aggarwal (2002) found that the lack of organizational support and involvement was a major source of stress reported by their sample of Ontario hospital nurses. This finding accords with results from a study that examined nurses working within a children's hospital (McGowan, 2001). An association was also found between the lack of managerial support and both negative mood states and low levels of work satisfaction among nurses (Bennett, Lowe, Matthews, Dourali, & Tattersall, 2001; Healy & McKay, 2000).

A German study discovered that compared to nurses who had a sense of personal control, nurses who believed they had minimal control over events in their lives were expected to experience increased vulnerability to stress and burnout (Schmitz, Nuemann, & Oppermann, 2000). To no surprise, it was anticipated that nurses who eventually experienced burnout would be less productive and provide a lower quality of care. This poor service could result in decreased patient satisfaction.

Physician Stress

An escalation in stress-related illnesses among Dutch physicians was identified following a survey of medical specialists regarding work-related stress and satisfaction (Visser, Smets, Oort, & de Haes, 2003). Results from this study indicated that levels of stress and satisfaction were best understood by respondents' perception of working conditions. More specifically, factors such as time pressure, restriction of professional autonomy, and job insecurity were mentioned.

According to Linzer, Gerrity, Douglas, McMurray, Williams, and Konard (2002), "Stress, burnout, depression and anxiety have been described in up to 25 percent of practicing physicians" (p. 38). In a study conducted by these authors, several factors that contributed to physician stress were identified and included solo practice, time pressure, case mix, less control of the workplace, hassles, lack of collegial support for balancing work and home, isolation, complex patients, and time pressure during patient visits.

The literature regarding stress among doctors and dentists who held teaching positions was reviewed (Rutter, Herzberg, & Paice, 2002). It was determined that doctors and dentists with training or teaching responsibilities were no more stressed than their non–teaching/training counterparts. Interestingly, it appeared that teaching and training responsibilities helped to mitigate stress.

HIV/AIDS Medical Care. Attention regarding physician stress has been devoted to specialized areas of medicine. For example, Lert, Chastang, and Castano (2001) assessed the psychological stress among hospital doctors who cared for HIV patients. Results from this study indicated neither the length of time working in HIV/AIDS nor the proportion of HIV/

AIDS work was related to stress or satisfaction. On the other hand, the main predictors of psychological distress, emotional exhaustion, and depersonalization included work overload and stress derived from social relationships at work.

Child and Adolescent Psychiatry. Medical directors in child and adolescent psychiatry who assumed the dual role of clinician and manager experienced specific job-stressors (Kirkcaldy & Siefen, 2002). Physicians who participated in this study reported stress related to workload, personal responsibilities, management, and daily hassles.

Anesthesiology. The most common stressful aspects of anaesthetic medicine were identified as time constraints and interference with home life (Kluger, Townend, & Laidlaw, 2003). Issues relevant to time pressure included producing rapid patient turnover, travel between hospitals, and same-day admission intervention. In terms of gender differences, female anesthetists reported higher stress levels compared to their male counterparts. Kluger and colleagues (2003) hypothesized that female physicians were more involved in home life commitments, thus accounting for their higher stress level.

Some root causes and eventual consequences of physician stress were discussed by Menninger (cited in Lamberg, 1999). According to Menninger, personality traits that helped physicians succeed in medical school and prosper in their professional careers may eventually undermine their overall happiness. Menninger went on to address physician impairment and its potential fallout.

Police Officer Stress

There exist many long-standing beliefs (Curran, 2003) and contradicting reports within police stress research (Le Scanff & Taugis, 2002; Patterson, 2002; Shipley & Baranski, 2002). In an effort to organize information, Abdollahi (2002) provided a detailed review of the literature and categorized the different types of stressors. The categories included intra- interpersonal, occupational, organizational, and health.

Several popular myths regarding police stress have been debunked (Curran, 2003). To clarify the issue of police stress, Curran reviewed several themes including suicide rates, debriefing effectiveness, involvement in fatal events and psychological recovery, occupation dangerousness, alcohol consumption, and divorce. Similarly, Zhao, He, and Lovrich (2002) dispelled the notion that police work was highly dangerous. These researchers wrote,

... it seems that the work environment in law enforcement is not as highly dangerous as commonly believed because the use of deadly force and the incidence of highly dangerous situations are rather infrequent in most jurisdictions. Although the media tend to portray police work as dangerous, their examples tend to be drawn from inner-city settings where drug enforcement is visible or from the rare incidences of school violence or multiple-murder crime scenes. (p. 56)

More specific investigations into various aspects of police work have been explored. Gershon, Lin, and Li (2002), for example, examined the issue of age in relationship to stress among police officers. These authors discovered that "... older officers with higher levels of work stress are at significant risk of serious physical, mental, and health risk problems" (p. 164). Two key work-related stressful events reported by officers included needlestick injuries and police funerals. Zhao and colleagues (2002) examined sources of stress within the organizational setting and discovered that, in general, officers did not "... view the environment at their workplace in a particularly negative light" (p. 51). Interesting findings included the association between higher levels of education and stress and the adverse impact of bureaucracy on officer stress.

Stress among municipal police officers who performed a relatively risk-free job has been studied (Pancheri et al., 2002). Results suggested that officers who were actively involved in traffic control appeared to react more maladaptively than officers who performed office jobs. Another finding from this research suggested women appeared to present more stress than men.

The dearth of information regarding the experiences of women in policing has been underscored and factors that contribute to different levels of stress between male and female officers have been identified (Thompson, Kirk-Brown, & Brown, 2001). It was determined that female officers share the same sources of stress as their male counterparts. Gender discrimination, however, was a significant source of stress and was likely to affect family relationships.

Four major categories of law enforcement stressful events include external, internal, task-related, and individual (Patterson, 2001). External events occurred outside the law enforcement organization/bureaucracy (e.g., negative media portrayals of law enforcement officers). Internal events occurred within the organization or bureaucracy (e.g., inadequate pay, training, support). Task-related events occurred on the job (e.g., role conflicts, shift work). Finally, individual events included life events (e.g., working a second job, parenting problems, health issues).

While acknowledging the aforementioned categories, Patterson (2001) argued that *traumatic events* should be included as an additional category.

Traumatic events were described as incidents involving (1) injury to self or others, (2) major disasters, and (3) controlling public disorders. While acknowledging that traumatic events may occur infrequently, Patterson suggested a potential link between stress and more serious emotional repercussions and wrote,

> Recognizing a comprehensive classification of stressful work events and situations experienced by law enforcement personnel is important because the negative psychological effects of stress arising from various events may impinge on police officers' psychological well being to exacerbate the effects of a traumatic incident. (para. 12)

To ensure professional well-being, law enforcement organizations were encouraged to remain aware of the full range of events and situations experienced by police officers. Buchanan, Stephens, and Long (2001) echoed a similar recommendation regarding young police officers.

Correctional Officer Stress

Some sources of stress have worsened for correctional officers. Finn (1998) provided an outstanding literature review of this topic and considered organizational, work, and external factors. Organizational sources of stress included: understaffing, overtime, shift work, supervisor demands, role conflict, and role ambiguity. Work-related sources of stress included: threat of inmate violence, inmate violence, inmate demands and manipulation, problem with coworkers. External sources of stress included: low public recognition or image and poor pay.

The potential effects of stress on individuals and institutions were outlined by Childress, Talucci, and Wood (1999). These authors noted that officer stress can result in high staff turnover and eventual financial burdens on correctional institutions (e.g., worker compensation claims).

Probation Officer Stress

It was contended by Slate, Johnson, and Wells (2000) that minimal attention had been rendered to probation officer stress. To pique interest in this area, these authors provided a review of the extant research. Their review explored sources of officer stress and included potential questions for future research.

Firefighter Stress

The level of experienced stress among firefighters has been associated with problem-solving appraisals (Baker & Williams, 2001). Baker and Williams concluded that problem-solving appraisals served a moderating function between work stress and psychological distress. In other words, the timely fashion and manner in which these professionals confronted problems and engaged in problem solving influenced levels of personal stress.

Disaster Personnel Stress

Attention has been rendered to the personal reactions to emergency stress in employed and volunteer emergency workers who respond to disasters. Innes and Slack (1990) emphasized that "... there are wide differences between people in the reactions to stress" (p. 385) and repeatedly underlined the need for research. Following their review of the literature, they wondered about personality variables of volunteers and the issues of altruistic motivation, empathy, and methods of conflict resolution.

Volunteer Disaster Personnel Stress

In the study of rural volunteer emergency workers, Moran and Britton (1994) found, "Variables associated with emergency service work, length of service and number of callouts, were generally the most efficient predictors of reactions to traumatic incidents" (p. 583). When presenting their research, however, these authors were cautious not to generalize their findings to paid emergency workers since they typically respond to more callouts. Potential differences between rural and urban disaster workers was also noted.

Social Worker Stress

After reviewing the literature regarding social worker stress, Lloyd, King, and Chenoweth (2002) had two questions in mind: "Are social workers subject to greater stress than other health professionals?" and "What factors contribute to stress and burnout among social workers?" (p. 255). Their review indicated reports of social worker stress were primarily anecdotal and there was a tendency to contrast social worker stress with the general population norms rather than workers in comparable professions. These authors remarked,

From descriptive accounts, the literature has identified social work as being a profession that is at high risk of stress and burnout. The studies that have been conducted have revealed that social workers are experiencing stress and burnout, but the picture is unclear as to whether they experience more stress and burnout than comparable occupational groups. (p. 263)

It has been concluded that although the quantity and quality of empirical research is weak, social workers may experience high levels of stress and burnout (Lloyd et al., 2002). Factors that reportedly contributed to social worker stress included the discrepancy between the ideals of the social work profession and actual practice, the mental health status of the professional, and organizational issues (e.g., role conflict, role ambiguity, challenge of the job).

INTERVENTION

The recommended intervention for helping professional stress generally involves operational, contextual, and managerial consideration (Thompson, Kirk-Brown, & Brown, 2001). Operational sources of stress refer to tasks, contextual sources of stress refer to relationship/cultural factors, and managerial sources of stress refer to such issues as policies and workload. Similarly, Le Scanff and Taugis (2002) identified stress factors that were recognized at the organizational, group, and individual levels. While acknowledging this general template and outlining prevalent stress management strategies, Bennett and colleagues (2001) underscored the need to conduct "… a full stress audit and work with staff to develop idiosyncratic responses to particular organizational issues" (p. 62). In short, stress is unique to each individual.

When considering intervention, the issue of effectiveness remains critical and requires ongoing attention. Edwards and colleagues (2002), for example, provided a systematic review of stress management interventions. Albeit specific to mental health professionals, this overview presented valuable information and constructive commentary for future research. For example, these authors remarked that, due to the heterogeneity of studies, "It is impossible to determine which specific interventions or techniques are most effective and should be recommended" (p. 213). Edwards and Burnard (2003) completed a very impressive literature review and meta-analysis regarding stress and stress management interventions for mental health nurses. Finally, Anshel (2000) described a comprehensive coping model that involved stress detection, cognitive appraisal, approach/avoidance-coping dimensions, and cognitive/behavioral-coping subdimensions.

Levels of Intervention

As noted below, intervention can occur at the organizational, group, and individual levels. Although intervention at one level might benefit some individuals, it is more likely that effective intervention would include measures at each level.

Organizational. At the organizational level, Le Scanff and Taugis (2002) suggested several ideas including (1) reduced work load, (2) improved work conditions, (3) rewards and encouragement, (4) improved social climate, and (5) a place to express concerns. In addition to workload reduction, Kirkcaldy and Siefen (2002) encouraged task delegation, review groups, and leadership coaching. The notion of rewards, positive administrative feedback, and availability of resources and services was proposed by Visser and colleagues (2003). The idea of providing psychosocial intervention training in order to enhance nurse empathy was also put forth (Edwards & Burnard, 2003).

Group. Group intervention techniques included more time for employee emotional debriefing, simulation exercises to prepare for real situations, and short stress management exercises (Le Scanff & Taugis, 2002). Sharkey and Sharples (2003) described a team-based learning pact to encourage and develop collaborative working practice. The effectiveness of groups to decrease a sense of aloneness was emphasized by Lamberg (1999). Interestingly, Kluger and colleagues (2003) discovered that the presence of skilled assistance was the greatest factor in reducing stress.

Individual. Individual intervention techniques included stress management courses that might involve behavioral techniques, progressive relaxation techniques, concentration techniques, enhanced communication skills, and cognitive restructuring (Baker & Williams, 2001; Edwards & Burnard, 2003; Le Scanff & Taugis, 2002; Sowa & May, 1994). Along with others, Kirkcaldy and Siefen (2002) recommended time and stress management, professional educational programming, and brief sabbatical leaves. Wilson, Tinker, Becker, and Logan (2001) reviewed the value of EMDR (Eye Movement Desensitization and Reprocessing) and Pongruengphant and Tyson (2000) provided evidence that, "… compared to nurses who cry infrequently, emotional crying may benefit nurses with lower intrinsic job satisfaction" (p. 538).

Social, Coping, and Problem-Solving Skills

The need for social skills training is considered an important element in the treatment of stress. Schmitz, Neumann, and Oppermann (2000) suggested such training could improve interpersonal problem solving, practical skills, and contribute to enhanced locus of control. Along a similar vein, several authors (Baker & Williams, 2001; Healy & McKay, 2000; Tyson, Pongruengphant, & Aggarwal, 2002) recommended strategies that teach problem solving skills and increase a sense of employee self-control. Additional strategies included enhancing interpersonal communication and clinical skills (Escot et al., 2001) and the development of effective coping skills (Gershon, Lin, & Li, 2002).

Support

The importance of various forms of support has been acknowledged. Moreover, it has been suggested that the social support of colleagues could provide a safety net. Various forms of social support include: organizational (Bennett et al., 2001; Sowa & May, 1994), collegial (Coffey & Coleman, 2001; Edwards et al., 2000; Gershon, Lin, & Li, 2002; Innes & Slack, 1990; Kluger et al., 2003; Lloyd, King, & Chenoweth, 2002), family (Callaghan, Tak-Ying, & Wyatt, 2000), supervisory (e.g., Kiemle, 1994; Lloyd, King, & Chenoweth, 2002; Sowa & May, 1994), and mentoring (Sowa & May, 1994).

Staff and Management Collaboration

The critical role of management in staff stress reduction resounds throughout the literature.

Coffey (1999) described the need for supportive attitudes and mechanisms between management and staff. For example, Coffey suggested reducing staff isolation and increasing joint decision-making. Bennett and colleagues (2001) also commented on the potential benefits associated with staff-management contact and the validation of staff.

SUMMARY

The defining features of stress are vague, and a specific timeline has not been established. According to the literature, a stress diagnosis simply requires that events or threats exceed an individual's *estimated coping* mechanism.

Despite a lack of clarity, stress remains an established construct that is supported by a large body of literature. Interest in stress is particularly evident within various specialties of nursing. Further, noteworthy attention has been rendered to the controversial issue of police stress. As a result of its historical popularity, a wide range of evaluation resources and intervention strategies accompanies the stress construct. For example, evaluation material includes structured interviews, diagnostic questionnaires, and inventories. The area of intervention is also comprehensive and addresses various needs at the individual, group, and organization levels.

Not surprisingly, this construct also boasts an impressive information resource list that includes books and journals. Several organizations have also been established and are devoted to the dissemination of information regarding stress.

EVALUATION RESOURCES

Structured Interviews

The Structured Event Probe and Narrative Rating Method for Measuring Stressful Life Event
Dohrenwend, B., Raphael, K., Schwartz, S., Stueve, A., & Skodol, A. (1993). In L. Goldberger & S. Breznitz (Eds.), *Handbook of stress: Theoretical and clinical aspects* (2nd ed.), pp. 174–199. New York: Free Press.

Stress Interview
Friedman, M., & Rosenman, R. (1959). Association of specific overt behavior pattern with blood and cardiovascular findings. *Journal of the American Medical Association, 169,* 1286–1296.

Diagnostic Questionnaires

The Coping Resources Inventory for Stress: A Comprehensive Measure of Resources for Stress-Coping
Matheny, K., Curlette, W., Aycock, D., Pugh, J., Pugh, J., & Taylor, H. (1987). *The coping resources inventory for stress.* Atlanta, GA: Health Prisms.

The Derogatis Stress Profile: A Theory-Driven Approach to Stress Management
Derogatis, L. (1987). The Derogatis Stress Profile DSP: Quantification of psychological stress. In G. Fva & T. Wise (Eds.), *Research Paradigms in Psychosomatic Medicine*, pp. 30–54. Basel: Karger.

Nurse Stress Index
Harris, P. (1989). The Nurse Stress Index. *Work and Stress, 3,* 335–346.

Occupational Stress Indicator
Cooper, C., Sloan, S., & Williams, S. (1988). *The Occupational Stress Indicator.* Windsor: NFER Nelson.

Stress Map
Orioli, E. (1987). *StressMap: Personal diary edition.* New York: Newmarket.

Stress Resiliency Profile: A Measure of Interpretive Styles That Contribute to Stress
Thomas, G, & Tymon, W. (1992). *Stress resiliency profile*. Tuxedo, NY: Xicom.

Stress Schedule
Hallberg, E., & Hallberg, K. (1986). *The stress schedule manual*. Sierra Madre, CA: Ombuds-man.

Inventories

Health Professional Stress Inventory (Revised Version)
Eells, T., Lacefiedl, P., & Maxey, J. (1994). Symptom correlates and factor structure of the health professions stress inventory. *Psychological Reports, 75,* 1563–1568.

Coping Inventory for Stressful Situations
Endler, N., & Parker, S. (1991). *Coping inventory for stressful situations: Manual.* Toronto, ON: Multi-Health Systems.

Daily Stress Inventory
Brantley, P., & Jones, G. (1989). *The Daily Stress Inventory: Professional manual.* Odessa: FL: Psychological Assessment Resources.

Life Stressors and Social Resources Inventory: A Measure of Adults' and Youths' Life Concerns
Moss, R., & Moss, B. (1994b). *Life stressors and social resources inventory youth form manual.* Odessa, FL: Psychological Assessment Resources

The Global Inventory of Stress
Radmacher, S., & Sheridan, C. (1989). The global inventory of stress: A comprehensive approach to stress assessment. *Medical Psychotherapy: An International Journal, 2,* 75–80.

INFORMATION RESOURCES

Books

David, M., & McKay, M. (1999). *The relaxation and stress reduction workbook* (4th ed.). Oakland, CA: New Harbinger.
Dryden, W. (1994). *The stresses of counselling in action.* Thousand Oaks, CA: Sage.
Goldberger, L., & Breznitz, S. (Eds.). (1993). *Handbook of stress: Theoretical and clinical aspects* (2nd ed.). New York: Free Press.
Olshevski, J., Katz, A., & Knight, B. (1999). *Stress reduction for caregivers.* Philadelphia, PA: Brunner/Routledge.
Palmer, S., & Dryden, W. (Eds.). (1996). *Stress management and counselling: Theory, practice, research, and methodology.* London: Cassell.
Quick, J., Murphy, L., & Hurrell, J. (Eds.). (1992). *Stress and well being at work: Assessments and interventions for occupational mental health.* Washington, D.C.: American Psychological Association.
Varma, V. (Ed.). (1997). *Stress in psychotherapists.* New York: Routledge.

Zalaquett, C., & Wood, R. (Eds.). (1998). *Evaluating stress: A book of resources* (2nd ed.) Lanham: MD: Scarecrow Press.

Zalaquett, C., & Wood, R. (Eds.). (1997). *Evaluating stress: A book of resources*. Lanham, MD: Scarecrow Press.

Journals

Anxiety, Stress, and Coping. http://www.tandf.co.uk/journals/alphalist.html.

International Journal of Stress Management. http://www.isma.org.uk.

Stress and Health: Journal of the International Society for the Investigation of Stress. http://www3.interscience.wiley.com/cgi-bin/issuetoc?ID=85513140.

Stress Medicine. http://www3.interscience.wiley.com/cgi-bin/issuetoc?ID=73504771.

Related Organizations

International Stress Management Association. URL: http://www.isma.org.uk.

The American Institute of Stress. URL: http://www.stress.org.

3

Acute Stress Disorder

Although having worked within the ambulance service for several years, Alana was stunned by what she observed when arriving at the scene of a school bus accident. The sight and sound of injured children screaming and crying temporarily stunned her. Despite this initial reaction, Alana was able to act swiftly and stabilize children who were removed from the overturned vehicle.

Days following the accident, the heroic efforts of Alana and her colleagues were acknowledged and celebrated in newspapers and on the television. Parents, local citizens, and school authorities praised the rapid response and courage of rescue workers who worked through dreadful conditions. Like her colleagues, Alana was proud of her skills and ability to assist the youngsters. Nevertheless, she struggled with feelings of detachment and emotional unresponsiveness days after the accident. Alana became agitated when family or friends recounted specific details of the tragedy and tried to engage her in conversation about her experience.

During one incident, Alana reacted abruptly toward her son's daycare worker after being thanked for her efforts. Unlike Alana, she was also less active with her son after work and insisted that he play alone quietly. Her son's sudden burst of laughter or shouting would easily startle Alana and she would find herself reprimanding the youngster for what she once considered normal behavior.

Alana and her colleagues realized that her disposition and behavior was out of character. She appeared usually tired, frustrated, and restless. Concerned about her health, Alana made arrangements to visit her family physician for her unexplained symptoms.

CONSTRUCT OVERVIEW

Acute stress "… is the development of characteristic anxiety, dissociative, and other symptoms that occurs within 1 month after exposure to an extreme traumatic stressor" (American Psychiatric Association, 2000, p. 429). An individual who has been exposed to a traumatic event develops anxiety symptoms, reexperiences the event, and avoids stimuli related to the event for less than four weeks afterward may be suffering from this anxiety disorder.

Bryant and Harvey (2000, 1997) and Bryant (2000) traced the historical development of acute stress disorder (ASD) and provided a comprehensive review. According to these authors, a formal diagnosis of ASD was first introduced in the *Diagnostic and Statistical Manual for Mental Disorders* (American Psychiatric Association, 1994). They also pointed out that ASD remains in its infancy and that many of the beliefs about ASD lack empirical evidence. As a matter of fact, a great deal of controversy surrounding the ASD diagnosis persists (e.g., Koopman, 2000). For example, Harvey and Bryant (2002) concluded that the theoretical and empirical support for ASD is flawed and that "… there is little justification for the ASD diagnosis in its present form" (p. 886). They further stated: "The available evidence indicates that alternative means of conceptualizing acute trauma reactions and identifying acutely traumatized people who are at risk of developing PTSD need to be considered" (p. 886).

The criticisms directed toward the ASD diagnosis include: (1) dissociation as a necessary response to trauma, (2) the main role of an ASD diagnosis was to predict another diagnosis, (3) an ASD diagnosis may pathologize transient stress reactions, (4) differentiating between two diagnoses that share similar symptoms on the basis of symptom duration, and (5) insufficient empirical evidence to support ASD (Harvey & Bryant, 2002).

AFFECTED POPULATIONS

As demonstrated below, information regarding acute stress disorder among helping professionals has been limited to police officers and rescue workers.

Police Officer Acute Stress Disorder

Police officer performance under conditions of acute stress has been explored. More specifically, Shipley and Baranski (2002) sought to improve the performance of police officers "… in critical, combative, and

TABLE 3.1
Acute Stress Symptomatology

Emotional	Cognitive	Physical	Behavioral
Fear	Dissociative amnesia	Reduced awareness	Avoidance of stimuli that arouse recollections of the trauma
Horror		Increased arousal	Motor restlessness
Helplessness	Derealization	Difficulty sleeping	Impairment in social, occupational, or other important areas of functioning
Emotional Numbing	Depersonalization Distress on exposure to reminders of the traumatic event	Hypervigilance Exaggerated startle response	
Detachment	Sense of reliving the experience	Recurrent images, thoughts, dreams, illusions, flashback episodes	
Absence of emotional responsiveness Anxiety Irritability	Poor concentration		

Adapted from American Psychiatric Association (2000). *Diagnostic and statistical manual of mental disorders*. Washington, DC, Author.

highly stressful situations" (p. 78). Findings from this study indicated participants who received the visuo-motor behavior rehearsal method displayed significantly lower anxiety scores and exhibited better performance on the critical incident event scenario.

Rescue Worker Acute Stress Disorder

A study was conducted to identify the characteristics and course of early stress response in a group of young, untrained military personnel (Yeh, Leckman, Wan, Shiah, & Lu, 2002). Results from this investigation suggested: "Young military personnel without formal training in rescue operations are at risk for ASD. But their risk appears to be no higher than generally reported for either trained rescue workers or victims in the general population" (p. 66).

INTERVENTION

In discussing intervention, Harvey and Bryant (2002) remarked that strategies are designed to minimize subsequent posttraumatic stress disorder. Specific strategies that were outlined included aspects of cognitive behavioral therapy (CBT) such as prolonged exposure, anxiety management, in vivo exposure, and cognitive therapy.

In their discussion of intervention, these authors drew an important distinction between *intervention* and *psychological debriefing* and wrote,

> It must be emphasized that the early intervention described here is qualitatively different to *psychological debriefing*, an intervention that has been popular in recent years. The early intervention is five to six sessions of CBT that are administered individually and only to carefully selected and highly symptomatic patients (those with ASD). The intervention typically commences at 2 weeks posttrauma and includes exposure, cognitive therapy, and anxiety management. (p. 897)

SUMMARY

A useful characteristic of acute stress is the specific timeline that defines this disorder. According to the DSM (American Psychiatric Association, 2000), a diagnosis of acute stress disorder requires individuals must demonstrate symptoms within 1 *month* of a traumatic event. A diagnosis of acute stress disorder also requires exposure to an *extreme* traumatic stressor.

It is remarkable, however, that despite appearing in the DSM-IV-TR, acute stress disorder has received so little attention. In fact, information is limited to the experiences of police officers and rescue workers. Furthermore, with the exception of one text and a handful of articles, there is an obvious absence of information regarding this disorder.

The lack of consideration regarding acute stress disorder is also evident in the areas of evaluation and intervention wherein there exist limited instruments and strategies. Finally, a specific journal or organization has not been devoted to the advancing knowledge regarding this disorder.

EVALUATION RESOURCES

Structured Interviews

Acute Stress Disorder Interview (ASDI)

Bryant, A., & Harvey, A. (2000). *Acute stress disorder: A handbook of theory, assessment, and treatment.* Washington, DC: American Psychological Association.

Bryant, R., Harvey, A., Dang, S., & Sackville, T. (1998). Assessing acute stress disorder: Psychometric properties of a structured clinical interview. *Psychological Assessment, 10,* 215–220.

Structured Clinical Interview for DSM-IV Dissociative Disorders (SCI-D)

Bryant, A., & Harvey, A. (2000). *Acute stress disorder: A handbook of theory, assessment, and treatment.* Washington, DC: American Psychological Association.

Cardena, E., Classen, C., & Spiegel, D. (1991). *Stanford acute stress reaction questionnaire.* Stanford, CA: Stanford University Medical School.

Steinberg, M. (1993). *Structured clinical interview for DSM-IV dissociative disorders (SCID-D).* Washington, DC: American Psychiatric Association.

Diagnostic Questionnaires

Stanford Acute Stress Reaction Questionnaire (SASRQ)

Bryant, A., & Harvey, A. (2000). *Acute stress disorder: A handbook of theory, assessment, and treatment.* Washington, DC: American Psychological Association.

Cardena, E., Classen, C., & Spiegel, D. (1991). *Stanford acute stress reaction questionnaire.* Stanford, CA: Stanford University Medical School.

Scales

Acute Stress Disorder Scale (ASDS)

Bryant, A., & Harvey, A. (2000). *Acute stress disorder: A handbook of theory, assessment, and treatment.* Washington, DC: American Psychological Association.

Bryant, R., Moulds, M., & Guthrie, R. (2000). Acute stress disorder scale: A self-report measure of acute stress disorder. *Psychological Assessment, 12,* 61–68.

INFORMATION RESOURCES

Books

Bryant, A., & Harvey, A. (2000). *Acute stress disorder: A handbook of theory, assessment, and treatment.* Washington, DC: American Psychological Association.

4

Posttraumatic Stress Disorder

Matthew was a popular team leader at a community group home for emotionally and behaviorally disturbed adolescents. He was always eager to help and welcomed new staff to the facility routines. Although he enjoyed working directly with the young people, Matthew was especially partial to crisis intervention strategies with high-risk children.

Matthew's view of his work drastically changed one afternoon when he witnessed a staff member being physically attacked and seriously injured by a resident. In recalling the event, Matthew remembered how helpless he felt when he saw a youngster run toward a female staff member, jump, and violently kick her in the back. After the staff member fell to the floor, the youngster began striking her head until he was restrained by the victim's colleagues.

Several weeks after the event, Matthew found himself easily startled and hypervigilant around the residents. Although the young person who had assaulted his colleague was dismissed from the group home and hospitalized, Matthew felt extremely vulnerable and insecure unless in the presence of a colleague. During his weekly supervision, Matthew's supervisor commented on his nervous laughter, elevated anxiety, and growing inflexibility with the children. Unable to explain his behavior change, Matthew discussed his shock when witnessing such unexpected and violent behavior. Matthew expressed the need to eliminate the recurrence of such events and insisted on increased resident restrictions.

CONSTRUCT OVERVIEW

As described in the *Diagnostic and Statistical Manual of Mental Disorders,* revised edition (American Psychiatric Association, 2000), posttraumatic stress disorder (PTSD) "… is the development of characteristic symptoms following exposure to an extreme traumatic stressor involving direct personal experience of an event that involves actual or threatened death or serious injury, or other threat to one's physical integrity or witnessing an event that involves death, injury, or a threat to the physical integrity of another person; or learning about unexpected or violent death, serious harm, or threat of death or injury experienced by a family member or other close associate" (p. 424).

It has been reported that PTSD was developed out of studies in combat neurosis, pathological grief, motor vehicle and industrial accidents, rape trauma, and emotional reactions that followed disasters (Daly, 1983). The long history of PTSD symptomatology goes back to the diary of Samuel Pepys and his ability to cope with the severe psychological trauma involving the Great Fire of London in 1666.

AFFECTED POPULATIONS

As demonstrated below, information regarding PTSD among helping professionals includes emergency room personnel, police officers, firefighters, rescue personnel, and emergency workers.

Emergency Room Personnel Posttraumatic Stress Disorder

Emergency room personnel posttraumatic stress symptoms, interpretations of traumatic events, and subsequent intrusive recollections, and peritraumatic dissociation were measured by Laposa and Alden (2003). Findings from this study suggested emergency room personnel were at increased risk for developing posttraumatic stress disorder. It was also determined that cognitive processes were critical in the disorder. In other words, there was an association between how individuals appraised the traumatic event and their level of symptomatology. A relationship between stress resulting from interpersonal conflict within the emergency department and PTSD symptomatology was also discovered (Laposa, Alden, & Fullerton, 2003).

Police Officer Posttraumatic Stress Disorder

Posttraumatic stress disorder symptoms among police officers 18 months after a rescue operation were explored (Renck, Weisaeth, & Skarbo, 2002). Results from this study showed the police officers were affected by their experience. Specific findings included: more female officers compared to male officers reported intrusive thoughts, older and single officers reported more intrusive thoughts compared to married or

TABLE 4.1
Posttraumatic Stress Disorder Symptomatology

Emotional	Cognitive	Physical	Behavioral
Intense fear	Recurring and intrusive distressing recollections of the traumatic event	Recurrent distressing dreams	Disorganized behavior
Horror	Thought avoidance associated with the traumatic event	Dissociative state	Persistent avoidance of stimuli related to the traumatic event
Distress	Amnesia	Physiological reactivity	Avoidance of conversation related to traumatic event
Emotional numbing	Difficulty concentrating	Sleeping problems	Increased arousal
Emotional avoidance	Inability to recall aspects of the traumatic event	Nightmares	Diminished responsiveness to external world
Feeling detached from people	Sense of a foreshortened future	Illusions	Diminished interest in previously enjoyed activities
Reduced ability to feel emotions	Difficulty completing tasks	Hallucinations	Hypervigilance
Increased anxiety	Flashback episodes		Exaggerated startle response
Irritability			Agitated
Helplessness			Anger outbursts

Adapted from American Psychiatric Association. (2000). *Diagnostic and statistical manual of mental disorders.* Washington, DC: Author.

cohabiting officers. Finally, officers who experienced other traumatic life events after the rescue reported more intrusive thoughts.

Researchers at the San Francisco Veterans Affairs Medical Center reported, "Police officers are more likely to suffer from posttraumatic stress disorder (PTSD) if they experience high levels of emotional distress, including panic reactions, at the time of traumatic events, such as a partner being injured or killed or their own life being threatened" (Kohn, Hasty, & Henderson, 2002, p. 6).

Violanti (2001) wondered about the efficacy of programs designed to assist police officers to deal with traumatic events. In doing so, he challenged what he considered to be pathogenic approaches that tend to script police officers into traumatic symptoms. Rather than adhering to a pathogenic approach, Violanti suggested intervenors view police officers as resilient active agents in their healing process with a focus on their positive strength and ability to grow.

In summary, Violanti remarked,

> Individuals should be allowed to make their own appraisal of just how sick they are when exposed to trauma. Police agency policy that mandates attendance at PTSD debriefings should not exist. Attendance should most certainly be voluntary, based on the officer's own decision of just how affected he or she is by the traumatic exposure. (para. 28)

The complexity of PTSD was further addressed by Saakvitne, Tennen, and Affleck (1998). In their critique, these authors emphasized the difficulty in formulating and assessing an individual's response to trauma and wrote, "The myriad intrapsychic, behavioral, somatic, interpersonal and subjective responses create both conceptual and methodological quandaries" (p. 280).

Firefighter Posttraumatic Stress Disorder

The assessment of firefighters following the Oklahoma City bombing was conducted by North and colleagues (2002a, b). Despite the horrific sights and enormous tasks of these professionals, there was no indication of significantly elevated rates of PTSD or impairment in functioning. They stated, "On average, study participants indicated the disaster experience heightened their job satisfaction, possibly by allowing them to demonstrate their competency and provide services for which they were selected and trained" (North et al. 2002a, p. 175). It was also discovered firefighters reported less PTSD compared to direct bomb blast survivors.

These findings contrast with Wagner, Heinrichs, and Ehlert (1998) who found that the firefighters in their sample often failed to cope with primary and secondary stress. These authors noted the personal (e.g., psychological) and systemic (e.g., absenteeism) consequences of this response.

It was pointed out that firefighters are exposed to two different PTSD risk factors that include life-threatening situations and grief, and the tragedies that can be associated with their work. This study revealed that the number of years on the job and the number of distressing missions were valid predictors of PTSD.

Rescue Personnel Posttraumatic Stress Disorder

McCammon, Durham, Allison, and Williamson (1988) conducted a study that included 53 police officers and fire-rescue workers and 26 hospital employees who responded to victims of two traumatic events. Results confirmed the belief that "… disastrous events involving extensive human suffering have lingering psychological impact on many emergency workers" (p. 365).

In their study of 79 rescue, medical personnel, and police officers, Durham, McCammon, and Allison (1985) reported that 80 percent of participants had at least one symptom of PTSD. According to these authors, intrusive thoughts was the most frequently reported symptom.

As might be expected, on-the-scene rescue workers reported more symptoms when compared to in-hospital staff.

Emergency Worker Posttraumatic Stress Disorder

The need to better understand the effect of PTSD on interpersonal relationships among emergency workers has been identified. McFarlane and Bookless (2001) surveyed the literature, noted the lack of research in this particular area, and concluded that a traumatic experience can impair key and potentially supportive interpersonal relationships.

INTERVENTION

The position that individuals deal with life adversities in their own unique way underpins PTSD intervention (Violanti, 2001). As discussed below, although several methods are advocated, the needs of each individual must be carefully considered and respected. Violanti wrote, "In sum, trauma, individual appraisal, coping, and psychological well-being all occur in a dynamic transactional relationship (Lazarus & Folkman, 1984). This is contrary to the static and rigid nature of present enduring pathogenic PTSD intervention models" (para. 27). While acknowledging the aforementioned perspective, several interventions exist and are described below.

Individual

Individual intervention involves pretrauma preparation and the use of stress rehearsal and stress inoculation techniques (McCammon et al., 1988). The emphasis in a pretrauma program is placed on cognitive and affective preparation.

As pointed out by McCammon and colleagues (1988), psychological debriefing could occur either informally or formally. Within an informal context, helping professionals can be encouraged to speak with one another in order to process their experiences. Formal debriefing, on the other hand, would involve more established mechanisms. For example, Flannery (1999) suggested the Critical Incident Stress Management could be helpful in gathering facts and in creating a context where individuals could express difficult emotions.

Based on their research, Laposa and Alden (2003) asserted, "... the findings imply that treatment for PTSD would benefit from addressing cognitive processes. In particular, appraisal of the trauma, its sequela, and intrusive memories need to be targeted" (p. 63).

Saakvitne, Tennen, and Affleck (1998) proposed the constructivist self-development theory (CSDT). CSDT involves helping individuals adapt by identifying the personal meaning they associate with their trauma. Within this framework, emphasis is placed on personal growth as evidenced through "... a greater sense of meaning, self-compassion, perspective, and insight" (p. 295).

A combination of psycho-education, cognitive-behavioral therapy, and EMDR (Eye Movement Desensitization Reprocessing) was described by Kitchiner and Aylard (2002). According to these authors, a collaborative therapeutic relationship was critical to treatment. Finally, Marshall and Pierce (2000) discussed the potential of medication in the treatment of PTSD.

Group

McFarlane and Bookless (2001) considered the effect of PTSD on interpersonal relationships and remarked that

> ... most treatment modalities do not use the power of the interpersonal domain as the focus for restitution in PTSD. Treatment interventions need to address the fact that the symptoms of PTSD not only alter relationships but also can be regulated by relationships. This raises the question as to the potential for the use of interpersonal psychotherapy in the treatment of patients. (p. 266)

Organizational

Organizations have been deemed the most powerful aspect of intervention (McCammon et al., 1988). It was the opinion of these authors that organizations, "... must analyze tasks and training, deployment and supervision policies and procedures" (p. 370).

SUMMARY

A PTSD diagnosis carries with it a specific timeline and requires that individuals must demonstrate symptoms for more than 1 *month*. A distinguishing feature of PTSD is that symptomatology appears severe and extreme (e.g., intense fear, horror). Further, PTSD requires exposure to an *extreme* traumatic stressor.

The amount of literature and assessment resources pertaining to PTSD is impressive and perhaps reflects its long history. Despite this acknowledgment, however, one cannot help but notice that little information exists regarding the experience of PTSD among helping professionals.

Comparable to stress, PTSD is accompanied by a wealth of information regarding evaluation and intervention strategies that consider individual, group, and organizational factors. Readers who are interested in learning more about this construct have access to a research quarterly, books, and organizations.

EVALUATION RESOURCES

Structured Interviews

Posttraumatic Stress Disorder Interview

Watson, C., Juba, M., Manifold, V., Kucala, T., & Anderson, P. (1991). The PTSD interview: Rationale, description, reliability, and concurrent validity of a DSM-III-based technique. *Journal of Clinical Psychology, 47*, 179–188.

Structured Interview for PTSD (SI-PTSD)

Davidson, J., Smith, R., & Kudler, H. (1989). Validity and reliability of the DSM-III criteria for post traumatic stress disorder: Experience with a structured interview. *Journal of Nervous and Mental Disorders, 177*, 336–341.

The Boston Clinical Interview for Posttraumatic Stress Disorder

Gerardi, R., & Wolfe, J. (1989). Boston clinical interview for PTSD. Boston: National Center for PTSD, Behavioral Science Division.

Questionnaires

Harvard Trauma Questionnaire

Mollica, R., Wyshak, G., DeMarneffe, D., Khuon, F., & Lavelle, J. (1987). Indochinese versions of the Hopkins Symptom Checklist-25: A screening instrument for the psychiatric care of refugees. *American Journal of Psychiatry, 144*, 497–500.

Distressing Event Questionnaire

Kubany, E., Leisen, M., Kaplan, A., & Kelly, M. (2000). Validation of a brief measure of posttraumatic stress disorder: The Distressing Event Questionnaire (DEQ). *Psychological Assessment, 12*, 197–209.

Purdue PTSD Questionnaire

Lauterbach, D., & Vrana, S. (1996). Three studies on the reliability and validity of a self-report measure of posttraumatic stress disorder. *Assessment, 3*, 17–25.

Traumatic Stress Schedule

Norris, F. (1990). Screening for traumatic stress: A scale for use in the general population. *Journal of Applied Social Psychology, 20*, 1704–1718.

Inventories

Trauma Symptom Inventory

Briere, J. (1996). *Trauma Symptom Inventory professional manual.* Odessa, FL: Psychological
    Assessment Resources.

Penn Inventory for Posttraumatic Stress Disorder

Hammarberg, M. (1992). Penn Inventory for post-traumatic stress disorder: Psychometric
    properties. *Psychological Assessment, 4, 67–76.*

Scales

Allodi Trauma Scale

Allodi, F. (1985). Physical and psychiatric effects of torture: Canadian study. In E. Stover
    and E. Nightingale (Eds.), *The breaking of bodies and minds: Torture, psychiatric abuses
    and the health professions.* New York: W. H. Freeman.

Clinician-Administered Posttraumatic Stress Disorder Scale

Blake, W., Weathers, P., & Nagy, R. (1990). *Clinician-administered PTSD scale (CAPS).* Boston:
    National Center for PTSD, Behavioral Science Division.

Impact of Event Scale-Revised (IES-R)

Weiss, D., & Marmar, C. (1996). The Impact of Even Scale-Revised. In J. Wilson & T. Keane
    (Eds.), *Assessing psychological trauma and PTSD* (pp. 399–411). New York: Guilford.

Los Angeles Symptom Checklist (LASC)

King, L., King, D., Leskin, G., & Foy, D. (1995). The Los Angeles Symptom Checklist: A self-
    report measure of posttraumatic stress disorder. *Assessment, 2, 1–17.*

Keane PTSD Scale of the MMPI (PK Scale)

Keane, T., Malloy, P., & Fairbank, J. (1984). Empirical development of an MMPI subscale for
    the assessment of combat-related post-traumatic stress disorder. *Journal of Consulting
    and Clinical Psychology, 52, 888–891.*

Mississippi Scale for Combat-Related PTSD

Keane, T., Caddel, J., & Taylor, K. (1988). Mississippi Scale for Combat-Related PTSD: Three
    studies in reliability and validity. *Journal of Consulting and Clinical Psychology, 56,*
    85–90.

Revised Civilian Mississippi Scale for PTSD

Norris, F., & Perilla, J. (1996). The revised Civilian Mississippi Scale for PTSD: Reliability,
    validity, and cross-language stability. *Journal of Traumatic Stress, 9, 285–298.*

The PTSD Scale of the SCL-90

Saunders, B., Mandoki, K., & Kilpatrick, D. (1990). Development of a crime-related post-
    traumatic stress disorder scale within the Symptom Checklist-90 Revised. *Journal of
    Traumatic Stress, 3, 439–448.*

Modified PTSD Symptom Scale: Self-Report Version (MPSS-SR)

Falsetti, S., Resnick, H., Resick, P., & Kilpatrick, D. (1993). The Modified PTSD Symptom Scale: A brief self-report measure of posttraumatic stress disorder. *The Behavioral Therapist, 16,* 161–162.

Posttraumatic Stress Diagnostic Scale (PDS)

Foa, E., Cashman, L., Jaycox, L., & Perry, K. (1997). The validation of a self-report measure of posttraumatic stress disorder. The Posttraumatic Diagnostic Scale. *Psychological Assessment, 9,* 445–451.

Checklists

PTSD Checklist — Civilian

Blanchard, E., Jones-Alexander, J., Buckley, T., & Fornesis, C. (1996). Psychometric properties of the PTSD Checklist (PCL). *Behavior Research and Therapy, 34,* 669–673.

INFORMATION RESOURCES

Books

Carlson, E. (1997). *Trauma assessments: A clinician's guide.* New York: Guilford.

Everstine, D., & Everstine, L. (1993). *The trauma response: Treatment for emotional injury.* New York: Norton.

Foa, E., Keane, T., & Friedman, M. (Eds.) (2000). *Effective treatments for PTSD: Practice guidelines from the International Society for Traumatic Stress Studies.* New York: Guilford.

Friedman, M. (2000). *Post traumatic stress disorder: The latest assessment and treatment strategies.* Kansas City, MO: Compact Clinicals.

Harvey, J., & Pauwels, B. (Eds.). (2000). *Post traumatic stress theory, research, and practice.* Philadelphia, PA: Brunner/Routledge.

Herman, J. (1992). *Trauma and recovery: The aftermath of violence—from domestic abuse to political terror.* New York: Basic Books.

Peterson, C., Prout, M., & Schwarz, R. (1991). *Post-traumatic stress disorder: A clinician's guidebook.* New York: Plenum.

Saigh, P., & Bremmer, D. (Eds.). (1998). *Post traumatic stress disorder: A comprehensive text.* Boston, MA: Allyn & Bacon.

Schiraldi, G. (2000). *The post traumatic stress sourcebook.* New York: McGraw-Hill

Scott, M., & Palmer, S. (1999). *Trauma and post-traumatic stress disorder counseling: A reader.* New York: Continuum International.

Scott, M., & Stradling, S. (1994). *Counselling for post-traumatic stress disorder.* London: Sage.

Tedeschi, R., & Calhoun, L. (1995). *Trauma and transformation: Growing in the aftermath of suffering.* Thousand Oaks, CA: Sage.

van der Kolk, B., Weisaeth, L., & McFarlane, A. (Eds.). (1996). *Traumatic stress.* New York: Guilford.

Waites, E. (1993). *Trauma and survival: Post-traumatic and dissociative disorders in women.* New York: Norton.

Williams, M., & Sommer, J. (Eds.). (1994). *Handbook of post-traumatic therapy.* Wesrtport, CT: Greenwood Press.

Wilson, J., & Raphael, B. (Eds.). (1992). *The international handbook of traumatic stress syndromes*. New York: Plenum.
Yule, W. (1999). *Post traumatic stress disorder: Concepts and therapy*. New York: Wiley & Sons.

Journals

Veterans Affairs National Center for PTSD Research Quarterly. URL: http://www.ncptsd.org/research/rq/index.html.

Related Organizations

National Center for Post-traumatic Stress Disorder. URL: http://www.ncptsd.org.
The International Society for Traumatic Stress Studies. URL: http://www.istss.org.

5

Compassion Fatigue/ Secondary Traumatic Stress Disorder

Jane, who was completing her first clinical rotation in a child and adolescent psychiatric unit, began to cry easily during seminar classes when other students were reviewing their clinical cases. Despite efforts to conceal her sadness, Jane's peers would frequently inquire about her emotional disposition. At first, Jane dismissed her behavior as just a "bad day" and thus was hesitant to share her despair. Over the course of a couple of weeks, however, Jane's peers remained persistent and, consequently, Jane slowly began to discuss her sadness about seeing children institutionalized and medicated. She went on to reveal that the stories she was hearing in class about adult patients who had been in long-term care contributed to her sense of gloom and despair for her young patients. She described her excessive worry and concern about the well-being and future of the children with whom she interacted. During her narrative, Jane expressed her anger toward the psychiatrists and her clinical supervisors. She felt that these professionals were abandoning the children who were entrusted to their care. Although Jane could not identify any actual inappropriate events, she believed the children deserved better care.

It became clear to the seminar leader and to Jane's peers that she was emotionally and physically exhausted and was absorbing patient pain. By her own admission Jane reported a dramatic decrease in appetite and normal exercise routine. As Jane stated, "she just didn't know what came over her."

CONSTRUCT OVERVIEW

O'Halloran (2001, para. 5) noted: "It is well established that individuals who encounter traumatic material or who work with traumatized clients can be profoundly impacted by their experiences." It has been further suggested by O'Halloran that mental health professionals can be affected cognitively (reduced concentration), emotionally (depression), or spiritually (anger toward God).

While discussing nurse burnout, Joinson (1992) was the first to use the term *compassion fatigue* (Salston & Figley, 2003). Later, Figley (1995b) coined the term secondary traumatic stress disorder (STSD). STSD is synonymous with the term compassion fatigue and has been defined as "… the natural consequent behaviors and emotion resulting from knowing about a traumatizing event experienced by a significant other — the stress resulting from helping or wanting to help a traumatized or suffering person" (Figley, 1995b, p. 7). Figley (2002) further elaborated,

> As psychotherapists we learn to be on the one hand objective and analytical in our professional role as helper. We must put our personal feelings aside and objectively evaluate our clients and administer the best treatments according to best practice guidelines. But on the other hand we cannot avoid our compassion and empathy. They provide the tools required in the art of human service. (p. 1433)

According to Figley (1995b), "STSD is a syndrome of symptoms nearly identical to PTSD, except that exposure to knowledge about a traumatizing event experienced by a significant other is associated with the set of STSD symptoms, and PTSD symptoms are directly connected to the sufferer, the person, experiencing primary traumatic stress" (p. 8). Figley (1995a) pointed out, "The difference between PTSD and STSD is that the latter can be more directly tied to the adjustment and recovery of the traumatized person: As the sufferer improves, the supporter experiencing STSD improves" (p. 571).

To delve deeper into the experiences of professionals who reported STSD, Raingruber and Kent (2003) conducted a qualitative study to explore the meanings associated with secondary trauma. In doing so, they examined the physical and perceptual signals experienced by professional caregivers. As noted by these authors, these sensations served as a Geiger counter that assisted professionals in assuming a reflective stance when trying to understand the traumatic event.

Distinctions between the diagnostic criteria for primary and secondary traumatic stress disorder appear in Table 5.2.

Figley (1995b) highlighted the scarcity of literature pertaining to helping professional compassion fatigue and STSD and identified factors

TABLE 5.1
Secondary Traumatic Stress Disorder Symptomatology

Emotional	Cognitive	Physical	Behavioral
Efforts to avoid feelings associated with traumatic event	Recollections of the traumatic event or traumatized person	Sleeping problems	Efforts to avoid activities associated with the traumatic event
Diminished affect	Sense of foreshortened future	Physiologic reactivity to cues	Efforts to avoid situations associated with the traumatic event
Irritability	Sudden reexperiencing of the traumatic event or traumatized person	Dreams of the traumatic event or traumatized person	Diminished interest in activities
	Reminders of traumatic event or traumatized person		Detachment from others
	Avoidance of thoughts associated with the traumatic event		Sudden outbursts of anger
	Psychogenic amnesia		Hypervigilance for traumatized person
	Difficulty concentrating		Exaggerated startle response

Adapted from Figley, C. (Ed.). (1995b). *Compassion fatigue: Coping with secondary traumatic stress disorder in those who treat the traumatized.* New York: Brunner/Mazel.

that contribute to helping professional trauma. Factors included (1) empathic responses, (2) personal traumatic experiences, (3) resurfacing of unresolved issues propelled by a victim's trauma, and (4) working with vulnerable populations.

In terms of counselor cognition, there may be a shift in beliefs, expectations, and assumptions. Dutton and Rubinstein (1995) also discussed witness guilt or clinician guilt whereby student nurses may "...feel guilty for enjoying life when she or he sees the struggle of a survivor" (p. 86). Despite the increased attention devoted to compassion fatigue, Figley (2002) asserted that there is a chronic lack of self-care among psychotherapists.

AFFECTED POPULATIONS

As demonstrated below, compassion fatigue/STSD has been reported within various helping professions and also within specialty areas (e.g., torture survivor counseling, child protective service).

TABLE 5.2

Suggested Distinctions between the Diagnostic Criteria for Primary and Secondary
Traumatic Stress Disorder

Symptom Type	Primary	Secondary
Stressor	Experienced an event outside the range of usual human experiences that would be markedly distressing to almost anyone, such as:	Helping victim who has experienced an event outside the range of usual human experiences that would be markedly distressing to most anyone such as:
	1. Serious threat to self	1. Serious threat to traumatized person (TP)
	2. Sudden destruction of one's environment	2. Sudden destruction to TP's environment
Reexperiencing	1. Recollections of event	1. Recollections of event/TP
	2. Dreams of event	2. Dreams of event/TP
	3. Sudden reexperiencing of event	3. Sudden reexperiencing of event/TP
	4. Distress of reminders of event	4. Reminders of TP/distressing event
Avoidance/ numbing of reminders	1. Efforts to avoid thoughts/feelings	1. Efforts to avoid thoughts/feelings
	2. Efforts to avoid activities/ situations	2. Efforts to avoid activities/situations
	3. Psychogenic amnesia	3. Psychogenic amnesia
	4. Diminished interest in significant activities	4. Diminished interest in significant activities
	5. Detachment/estrangements	5. Detachment/estrangements
	6. Diminished affect	6. Diminished affect
	7. Sense of foreshortened future	7. Sense of foreshortened future
Persistent arousal	1. Difficulty falling/staying asleep	1. Difficulty falling/staying asleep
	2. Irritability or outbursts of anger	2. Irritability or outbursts of anger
	3. Difficulty concentrating	3. Difficulty concentrating
	4. Hypervigilance for self	4. Hypervigilance for TP
	5. Exaggerated startle response	5. Exaggerated startle response
	6. Physiologic reactivity to cues	6. Physiologic reactivity to cues

Note: Symptoms under 1 month duration are considered normal, acute, crisis- related reactions. Those not manifesting until 6 months or more following the event are delayed posttraumatic stress disorder or secondary traumatic stress disorder.
Source: Adapted from Figley, C. (Ed.). (1995). *Compassion fatigue: Coping with secondary traumatic stress disorder in those who treat the traumatized.* New York: Brunner/Mazel.

Counselor Secondary Traumatic Stress Disorder

Trauma Survivor Counseling. A personal story was revealed by Hesse (2002) to emphasize the potential effects of trauma work. From her perspective, social work students were not receiving ample classroom instruction regarding trauma work. As a result, beginning professionals were unaware of secondary trauma. Hesse also discussed the potential effects of trauma on mental health workers as well as the manifestations of secondary trauma on professionals and clients.

Professionals who extend themselves to trauma survivors are included in the *secondary circle of trauma* (Inbar & Ganor, 2003). When referring to these professionals, these authors stated, "Their individual resilience is put to a maximum straining test when they witness terror and death on such a massive scale and on such a continuous basis" (p. 109). It was also pointed out that trauma professionals exert so much energy in helping others that they can sometimes neglect themselves.

Torture Survivor Counseling. The prevalence and severity of secondary traumatization in professionals who work with torture victims are unknown (Birck, 2002). To fill this void, Birck conducted an interesting study that involved 25 professionals working at the Treatment Center for Torture Victims in Berlin, Germany. Study participants included therapists (psychotherapists, physicians, and social workers), interpreters, and administration. Results from this study indicated compassion fatigue was low for interpreters and administrative employees and extremely high for therapists. Birck hypothesized that, "One reason for this finding may be that unlike interpreters, therapists have to write health certificates to reduce the risk of repatriation for patients" (p. 89). The threat of deportation was also identified as a significant risk factor for secondary traumatization among participants.

To their surprise, Birck and her colleagues discovered that, "Contrary to our expectations, high degree of personal satisfaction with work did not prevent secondary traumatization" (p. 89). However, compassion fatigue increased with the number of years in trauma work. It was suggested that, "Future studies should distinguish between different aspects of secondary traumatization" (p. 88).

Sexual Abuse Survivor Counseling. Due to high prevalence rates, counselors are likely to work with victims of sexual abuse (Jones, 2000). As such, counselors needed to remain cognizant of personal reactions when being with sexual abuse survivors and hearing their traumatic stories. According to Jones, if personal reactions are ignored, "... these reactions can impede therapeutic effectiveness and may even harm the client" (p. 379).

When describing the unique work of sexual abuse counselors, Jones underlined the impact that client disclosure can have on counselors. For instance, hearing about graphic accounts of abuse and learning about cruelty toward children can stir a myriad of emotions within the counselor (e.g., rage, shock, horror). Furthermore, clinical intervention with this client population may require extra effort in terms of establishing a trusting relationship, listening over and over again to stories of abuse, and dealing with one's own unresolved issues of childhood abuse. The overall effect that this type of work can have on counselors was encapsulated by Jones, who wrote:

> The shock and outrage of the reality that children are cruelly victimized can
> challenge world views and cause counselors to become cynical. Cynicism
> can affect the counseling relationship by leading counselors to disrespect
> survivor clients and lose faith in the process of treatment. (p. 385)

Attention has been devoted to the intense nature of crisis intervention and the predictors of secondary trauma in sexual assault trauma counselors (Ghahramanlou & Brodbeck, 2000). Although it was conceded that not all professional trauma counselors develop secondary trauma, several risk factors were found, including a positive personal trauma history, age, and work satisfaction. In their research, Ghahramanlou and Brodbeck underscored important distinctions between client contact type (e.g., emergency room counseling versus telephone hotline counseling) and the development of secondary trauma. These authors asserted that due to exposure differences, counselors who have direct client contact are at greater risk of secondary trauma. "Although hotline counselors also actively attend to a client's distress, the anonymous or *faceless* nature of telephone counseling is less likely to promote vicarious emotional processing of the trauma survivor's experience" (p. 231).

Sexual Abuse Perpetrator Counseling. A study was designed to explore secondary traumatic stress symptoms in a sample of counselors who worked with sexual abuse perpetrators (Steed & Bicknell, 2001). These authors discovered that professionals who worked with perpetrators of sexual abuse were negatively impacted and were at moderate or high risk of developing compassion fatigue. When explaining their results, these authors reported that new therapists were most at risk in terms of the avoidance variable. However, they further stated:

> It appears that, almost regardless of one's overall experience as a therapist,
> there is a common experience of being at considerable risk of STS when
> beginning work with perpetrators, this reducing somewhat by years two to
> four, then increasing again. (para. 21)

Based on this study, it was concluded that general clinical experience did not shield professionals against secondary traumatic stress and that fluctuating levels of secondary traumatic stress were a shared phenomenon.

Steed and Bicknell examined secondary traumatic stress symptomatology among therapists who work with sex offenders. In their literature review, these authors noted the disparity "... between the degree of therapist exposure to trauma-associated material and experiences of STS" (para. 6). More specifically, there are contradicting results regarding sexual abuse caseload and secondary traumatic stress. This discrepancy was attributed to the amount of time workers were exposed to trauma-based material per week or the overall amount of time workers are exposed to trauma-based material.

Results from Steed and Bicknell's preliminary study suggested that (1) working with sexual abuse offenders had a negative impact on helping professionals, and (2) new therapists who work with sexual perpetrators are most vulnerable.

Lay Counseling. A study of lay counselors indicated, that although participants experienced symptoms associated with secondary traumatic stress, "… the incidence of symptoms did not, on average, fall within the clinical range" (Ortlepp & Friedman, 2002, p. 219). It was hypothesized that the different work roles of participants and their limited involvement in trauma counseling situations served as buffering factors. Interestingly, when interviewed, participants reported personal growth and a greater connection with individuals.

Criminal Victim Counseling. Secondary traumatic stress in relation to professionals who work with victims of crime was discussed by Salston and Figley (2003). These authors provided a review of the extant literature regarding STS and related psychological injury constructs. This generic overview acknowledged the challenges associated with trauma work, the influence of a professional's trauma history, STS assessment and prevention, and the need for future research.

Counselor Education Counseling. The needs of prospective counselors has been addressed by O'Halloran (2001). When discussing secondary traumatic stress in the classroom, O'Halloran underscored the importance of "… anticipating and addressing the emotional difficulties students experience in graduate-level courses on trauma and violence" (para. 1). While underscoring the importance of preparing students, O'Halloran also pointed out that unresolved issues may be triggered and surface during lectures. As indicated in the literature (e.g., Alpert & Paulson, 1990; Pope & Feldman-Summers, 1992), professional psychotherapists generally feel that they did not possess the necessary skills and knowledge to work with trauma and, in particular, child abuse.

During the syllabus review, students can be socialized to counselor education and become informed about the potential emotional discomfort that can accompany this process. It should also be spelled out to students that informed consent is required and they cannot be required to place themselves in situations that might jeopardize their physical or emotional well-being. This socialization period forewarns students, and reminds educators about the need for established parameters and respect. An added advantage of such forewarning is that it underscores the parallel process between counselors and clients.

Nurse Secondary Traumatic Stress Disorder

In a study of the nursing profession, Joinson (1992) argued that the nursing profession sets up nurses for compassion fatigue and discussed three core issues that related to nursing and compassion fatigue. She wrote:

> (1) caregivers may perform a number of concrete functions, but the essential product they deliver is themselves. This can be very taxing. They have to renew themselves, bulking themselves back up, or they're in trouble. (2) Human need is infinite. Caregivers tend to feel *I can always give a little more* but sometimes they just can't help. (3) Caregivers fill multiple roles that can be psychologically conflicting. For instance, nurses may move from patient care to administrative tasks to planning and delegation, then to a crisis. They can lose a lot of energy shifting roles. (p. 118)

The unique context of nursing was also addressed by Joinson. She noted that working in an environment clouded by indifference and cynicism can sap one's energy and enthusiasm.

Interestingly, Joinson also remarked that the abilities that make nurses successful can also be very costly to them. For example, nurses are primed and can become accustomed to putting the needs of others first and, consequently, they can lose sight of their own stressors.

Physician Secondary Traumatic Stress Disorder

For the most part, physicians do not possess, nor do they receive training in understanding how they are affected by patient suffering (Milstein, Gerstenberger, & Barton, 2002). As a result, they believed that physicians may experience significant stress when they encounter unfavorable outcomes. These authors elaborated, "When physicians are basking in the glory of a diagnostic or therapeutic coup, their highs are often unmatchable. On the other hand, when their attempts fail, their cognitive, emotional, and spiritual angst may be overwhelming" (p. 920).

Pfifferling and Gilley (2000, para. 2) suggested that "… compassion-fatigued physicians continue to give themselves fully to their patients, finding it difficult to maintain a healthy balance of empathy and objectivity." These authors noted that physicians could be unaware of how to arrest a downward spiral and tend to work harder until they are completely depleted.

The growing emotional and physical demands experienced by physicians contribute to physician compassion fatigue. According to Pfifferling and Gilley,

> In the past, the connection that many family physicians shared with their patients gave them the replenishment they needed to cope with the stressors of practicing medicine. But today, increasing demands have caused some physicians to stop taking the time to appreciate the love, respect and appreciation that their patients want to share with them. (para. 5)

Medical Students. Helping prospective physicians understand the relationship between empathy and compassion fatigue was addressed by Huggard (2003) who asked, "What are the requirements of a medical education programme that will prepare doctors to manage the effects of processes such as compassion fatigue?" (p. 164). The challenge of balancing keen diagnostic and empathy skills was alluded to by Huggard who focused on the responsibility of health care organizations. "In *caring for the carers*, the challenge for health care organisations lies in developing respect and care for their employees in the same way that they require their employees to care for patients. In doing this, health care organisations will support and assist their employees in sustaining and further developing their humanism" (p. 164).

Family Therapist Secondary Traumatic Stress Disorder

The pervasive nature of trauma work can invade a family therapist's work and personal life. "The very nature of therapeutic work may as easily compound trauma and stress as provide a haven for the therapist. The privacy of therapists' lives can be both a blessing and a curse, allowing therapists to have a life away from their personal tragedy and can create opportunities and dangers" (Carbonell & Figley, 1996, p. 55). While specifically addressing the issue of boundaries, Carbonell and Figley proposed the following five questions that family therapists can ask themselves:

1. How will you know when you are attempting to meet your heightened need for closeness by becoming over-invested in your clients?
2. How do you know when you unintentionally solicit closeness by being overwhelmingly lenient or non-confrontive with clients?
3. How can you tell when you are avoiding issues with clients because they are upsetting to you?

4. Will you be able to tell when you are experiencing, during a session, shame, guilt, anger, and/or depression related more to your personal life than to client material?

5. How will you be able to tell when your judgement is consistently impaired?

Because of the nature and context of their work, family therapists may be especially vulnerable to secondary traumatic stress (Figley, 1995a). The extreme intensity inherent in family matters is considered a main source of STS among family therapists. Figley (1995a) wrote, "No matter how hard they try to resist, family therapists are drawn into this intensity" (p. 575).

Three additional reasons why family therapists are especially vulnerable to STS have been identified by Figley (1995a). First, due to the context of family treatment, therapists are expected to maintain confidentiality, neutrality, and mutual support while working with victims and perpetrators who are from the same family system. In essence, maintaining a balanced perspective can be particularly challenging. Second, learning about family traumatic events can reactivate unresolved therapist trauma. As therapists learn about horrific events, old wounds can reopen. Finally, therapist empathy can contribute to STS. As noted by Figley, "... the process of empathizing with a traumatized person helps the therapist understand the person's experience of being traumatized, but, in the process, the therapist may be traumatized as well" (p. 575).

Correction Officer Secondary Traumatic Stress Disorder

Correction officers who empathize with individuals who suffer can experience a self-perpetuating cycle of cynicism and emotional depletion. Janik (1995, para. 2) wrote,

> Corrections professionals often hear offenders describe their troubling emotions, ideas, memories, fantasies and images. Although these graphic descriptions are severe, emotional catharses can be overwhelming and frightening, correction officers dare not communicate the wish to *turn away* from the horror of an inmate's experience for fear that the inmate might withdraw and despair that even a trained professional cannot help them.

The following interview excerpt was provided by Janik and illustrates the atrocious narrative accounts encountered by corrections officers.

> The first psychiatric patient I interviewed at the Cook County (Ill.) Department of Corrections complained of depression stemming from his incarceration. During the interview, he described how, while he was growing up,

his brother frequently raped him. He then boasted of having killed three children under the age of 5 and graphically described the rape and murder of a 6-year-old girl. His words had a chilling effect, leaving me anxious about the adequacy of supervision for my 6-year-old daughter and altering my naïve sense of safety for myself and my family. (para. 1)

This excerpt depicts how helping professionals can be influenced at the most primary level. Listening to stories of human suffering can set into motion a process whereby helping professionals begin to question their core beliefs. Janik asserted, "Corrections officers who must carry the toxic and corrosive experiences of inmates may find that these poisonous ideas conflict with their reassuring assumptions about the world, which they use to console themselves and derive hope for a better tomorrow" (para. 11). As proposed by Janoff-Bulman (1985), three core beliefs that might be challenged by this traumatization are (1) personal vulnerability, (2) the positive view of oneself, and (3) that the world is meaningful and orderly. Figley (1995b) suggested helping professionals may absorb the pain of patients and may need assistance in coping with intrusive thoughts, nightmares, and generalized anxiety. He went on to introduce the process of *empathic induction* and remarked that health care professionals can be so emotionally aroused by patient trauma that they in turn experience emotional upset. Furthermore, people could become emotionally drained by caring so much that they could be adversely affected by their efforts. In essence, caregivers are traumatized by concern.

Social Worker Secondary Traumatic Stress Disorder

Geriatric Social Work. The unique stresses experienced by social workers who work with the elderly make them a high-risk group for compassion fatigue (Leon, Altholz, & Dziegielewski, 1999). Despite this fact, little attention has been devoted to the relationship between gerontological social work and compassion fatigue. According to Leon and colleagues,

... increased frustration over limited financial, social and medical services for the elderly, exposure to the developmental challenges inherent during the older years and the worker's countertransferential are salient issues faced by social workers who treat the elderly. Specific challenges of working with the elderly include, serving clients who suffer from chronic illness (both medical and mental health conditions) and the resulting problems that must be addressed based on these conditions; the labor-intensive yet short term nature of the helping relationship; abuse potential and worker feelings toward it, as well as, a general lack of services and increasing pressure to cut costs by utilizing home-based services. (p. 51)

In addition to the aforementioned challenges, the degree of dissatisfaction experienced by helping professionals, and their inability to disassociate from their work have been identified as important factors that can contribute to compassion fatigue. Due to the fragility of the elderly, their death can occur with little notice. Consequently, following a patient's sudden death, helping professionals are sometimes unprepared and may question whether their services were adequate.

Leon and colleagues further remarked that, "While trying to help the client, the worker is also forced to confront issues with regard to his or her aging, the aging process of loved ones, as well as issues surrounding mortality" (p. 48). During this reflective process, it has been suggested that a helping professional's personal perceptions of aging and dying can intrude on the helping relationship. For example, helping professionals may grapple with fears of mental illness, being helpless, and dependent upon others.

Child Welfare Work. Despite having to intervene and witness the effects of childhood abuse and neglect, Dane (2000) reported little information existed regarding the emotional impact of chronic exposure to trauma on child welfare workers. These authors utilized focus groups to gather data for an eventual training model. Themes from this study included: sadness, child fatalities, successful and difficult cases, organizational stress and burnout, and spiritual and religious beliefs.

Child Protective Service. Child protection service (CPS) professionals face difficult challenges and, as noted by Cornille and Woodward Meyers (1999, para. 7),

> CPS workers, however, are just as likely as crisis workers and psychotherapists to be directly exposed to a number of children's traumas and personal traumas on a daily basis throughout their careers. While interviewing child abuse victims or reading case files, CPS workers learn graphic details of violent events and are forced to acknowledge cruelty to children in society. While investigating reported abuse, workers are often placed in compromising situations that result in physical harm or threatened harm, thus further increasing their exposure to traumatic stressors.

Additional challenges experienced by child welfare workers were outlined by Nelson-Gardell and Harris (2003). These authors pointed out that child welfare professionals must assess whether abuse or neglect has occurred, establish contact with children who are in acute distress, and confront alleged perpetrators. These authors noted that despite these inherent challenges, researchers have not investigated STS with child welfare workers.

Rehabiliation Worker Secondary Traumatic Stress Disorder

The need for rehabilitation counselors to be empathically available to clients and significant others who are survivors of traumatic and chronic life-threatening disabilities has been underlined (Stebnicki, 2000). Consequently, these professionals are susceptible to empathy fatigue, which has been described as emotional secondary stress and grief reactions that result from helping interactions. Stebnicki commented that these professionals experience a state of emotional, mental, and physical exhaustion that occurs when a counselor's personal issues or wounds are triggered by their client's life stories and experience of chronic illness and disability. Stebnicki elaborated,

> Many rehabilitation professionals, who by ethical obligation must place the needs of their clients above their own, may experience the secondary stressors associated with having to be empathically available at an intensive level of service. Consequently, the counselor may have parallel feelings of loss and grief or experience some degree of countertransference that results as secondary traumatic stress. (para. 34)

School Personnel Secondary Traumatic Stress Disorder

Kees and Lashwood (1996) described teachers, counselors, and administrators as frontline trauma workers and, thus, individuals who must remain open to the affective needs of students. As such, these professionals must contend with emotional consequences associated with their work:

> The fact that students are dealing with numerous and serious stressors in their lives is not new information to those working in schools. From everyday stressors common to most students such as violence, death, and loss, students of all ages are dealing with primary and cumulative stress that can result in extensive secondary stress for the teachers, counselors, and administrators working with them. (Kees & Lashwood, 1996, p. 42)

When discussing the reactions of school personnel, Kees and Lashwood described the stages of stress first described by Hans Selye (1974). Selye identified three stages including the (1) alarm stage, (2) stage of resistance, and (3) stage of exhaustion.

During the alarm stage, helping professionals exhibit surprise or anxiety due to an unfamiliarity with the situation. The stage of resistance involves helping professional resistance wherein coping strategies and defense mechanisms are mobilized to deal with the situation. During this stage, the person is extremely alert to the stressor. Finally, should the stressor persist or if additional stressors develop, the helper might enter the third and final exhaustion stage. Within the exhaustion stage, the person generally experiences fatigue, apathy, and listlessness.

Syntoxic Response. The helping professional tries to ignore or tolerate the stressor. An example is listening to distraught students in a detached fashion.

Catatoxic or Fight Response. The helping professional attacks the stressor, e.g., providing students with advice, reading literature, or directing them to additional resources.

Flight Response. The helping professional tries to escape the stressor and the feelings the stressor generates. Rather than providing a context wherein students can briefly describe their trauma, an attempt is made to immediately distance oneself from the stressor. An example is initiating immediate referrals. Although referrals may be appropriate, the timing and perceived lack of support are critical considerations.

Kees and Lashwood (1996) elaborated on the concept of helping professional restimulation, retraumatization, or both. According to these authors, this concept is more likely to occur if helping professionals have recently experienced a situation similar to those experienced by students or if past issues remain unresolved. Restimulation or retraumatization can manifest physically (e.g., feeling tense, perspiration), emotionally (e.g., worry, frustration, anger), cognitively (e.g., increased pressure to solve the problem or reduce student stress), or behaviorally (e.g., providing immediate advice, recommending reading material). In short, the efforts of helping professionals to ameliorate the distress of students may actually be a desire to avoid or escape secondary traumatization.

INTERVENTION

From the outset, it should be noted that Figley (2002) has edited a book specific to helping professional secondary traumatic stress. Combined with the additional interventions that follow, this book provides helping professionals with a wide variety of intervention strategies. Figley (1995a) also provided a framework for treating STS. In doing so, he listed seven essential elements that included: (1) respect, (2) educate, (3) stabilize, (4) pamper, (5) empower, (6) calm, and (7) transfer.

It is recommended that consideration be given to trauma counselor age (Ghahramanlou & Brodbeck, 2000) and experience. Raingruber and Kent (2003) noted the difference in professional experience and stated, "Clinicians precepting new employees and educators should provide anticipatory guidance to beginning practitioners that it is normal to experience strong physical perceptions and sensory-based memories" (p. 466). This is an important distinction and underscores the fact that professionals may react differently and present with different needs at various levels of development. Steed and Bicknell (2001) pointed to the vulnerability of clinicians newest to the profession and the importance of organizational and collegial support. This advice is especially pertinent in light of Arvay's (2001) comment that, "To date, few counsellor graduate training programs in Canada offer education about psychological trauma. And even fewer address the risk involved for both the counsellor and client in doing this difficult work" (p. 291). To prepare prospective professionals, Dane (2000) was convinced that trauma content needed to be infused throughout the social work curriculum. Cloitre (1998) believed that, "The topic of empirically-supported treatments also raises the issue of the need for students to be educated about the current state of research in the trauma field" (p. 13). The sensitive nature of introducing difficult material into the classroom has been addressed by McCammon (1995).

In general, intervention has been recommended at various levels. Inbar and Ganor (2003), for example, suggested intervention fell into the following four categories: (1) individual, (2) professional, (3) cognitive-behavioral, and (4) systemic social-organizational.

Individual Level

Figley (2002) believed that self-soothing techniques were critical. At the individual level, personal balance was deemed important (Jones, 2000), and professionals were encouraged to regain basic time management and organization skills (Inbar & Ganor, 2003). The importance of physical and psychological self-care (Bride et al., 2003; Badger, 2001; Hesse, 2002; O'Halloran, 2001; Pfifferling & Gilley, 2000), spiritual self-care (Hesse, 2002; Jones, 2001), and perhaps personal psychotherapy (Badger, 2001; Janik, 1995) were essential when treating trauma victims. In order to maintain a sense of well-being, Hesse (2002) recommended a blend of rest, relaxation, and various recreational activities.

Professional Level

Intervention at the professional level included participation in workshops, supervision, and professional networks (Arvay, 2001; Bride et al., 2003; Badger, 2001; Ghahramanlou & Brodbeck, 2000; Inbar & Ganor, 2003; Hesse, 2002; Jones, 2000; Leon et al., 1999). The need for staff and peer support (Badger, 2001; Bride et al., 2003; Cornille & Woodward Meyers, 1999; Hesse, 2002; Jones, 2001) has not gone unnoticed.

Hesse (2002) commented that helping professionals would be wise to remember the type of work they do and recognize and accept STS. The value of humor (Inbar & Ganor, 2003), assertiveness training (Leon et al., 1999), establishing boundaries (Badger, 2001), and limiting personal caseload (Hesse, 2002; Leon et al., 1999) was mentioned.

Cognitive-Behavioral

Cognitive-behavioral intervention generally involves encouraging professionals to develop cognitive coping skills when under stress (Inbar & Ganor, 2002; Kees & Lashwood, 1996). For example, strategies could involve proper breathing (Kees & Lashwood, 1996) and reflective questioning (Badger, 2001; Raingruber & Kent, 2003). Badger (2001) also encouraged self-monitoring techniques, journaling, and positive thinking.

Systemic Social-Organizational

Systemic social-organizational intervention referred to

> ... an organizational culture that prevents the creation of burnout condi-
> tion, and encourages effective coping; developing a leadership style that
> promotes joint vision, creativity, problem solving; and developing social
> and professional support systems such as the *Buddy System*, where profes-
> sionals share their concerns and experiences with each other. (Inbar &
> Ganor, 2003, p. 111)

Raingruber and Kent (2003) stated that health care organizations had to discover methods by which employees could grow and learn from their clinical experiences. Hesse (2002) identified the need for safety and comfort in the workplace and discussed office design. Establishing a proactive organizational or team approach plan to deal with STS was emphasized.

Attention has been given to the merit of staff training and skill devel-opment in the area of STS (Bride et al., 2003; Cornille & Woodward Mey-ers, 1999; Leon et al., 1999; Ortlepp & Friedman, 2002). Nelson-Gardell and Harris (2003) suggested the occupational hazard of STS should be broached within staff development. As stated by Arvay (2001), "Manag-ers of community agencies need to be advised of the toll this work may take upon their employees and support should be given to agencies in their applications for adequate funding and resources to address this crit-ical issue" (p. 291).

Modified Stroop Procedure. A Modified Stroop Procedure can be used to assess the transmission of war experiences from parents to children (Motta et al., 1997). The Stroop procedure is well established with a long history (MacLeod, 1991). In short, participants of the original Stroop Procedure were asked

> ... to name the color ink in which words were printed and to ignore the word itself. The words were actually names of colors such as "RED" and "GREEN" and these words were printed in incompatible ink colors. For example, the word "RED" was printed in green ink and the correct response on viewing this stimulus was "GREEN." Typically, it takes longer to name colors when word meaning and ink color are incompatible than when the meaning and color coincide (Motta et al. 1997, p. 896).

The Modified Stroop Procedure essentially involved asking participants to name the colors of the words that were associated with the Vietnam War while not stating the words themselves. The purpose of the Modified Stroop test was to detect subtle psychological effects that may not be detected by standard trauma measures (e.g., Impact of Events Scale, Minnesota Multiphasic Personality Inventory).

SUMMARY

Comparable to acute stress disorder and posttraumatic stress disorder, STSD is accompanied by a specific timeline. As evidenced in the literature review, STSD has been explored within a number of helping professions. The same degree of interest, however, is not evident in the area of evaluation. Presently, two questionnaires and one scale have been designed to assess STSD. The growing body of STSD literature is accompanied by books, a specific journal, and an institute.

It should also be considered that "There is evidence that individuals can develop strong, negative emotional reactions simply by enduring the stress of a close, personal relationship with someone who has been traumatized" (Motta, Kefer, Hertz, & Hafeez, 1999, p. 1001). Despite this evidence, however, these authors report that there are few ways in which to assess secondary stress disorder and existing methods are limited to specific populations. Motta and colleagues (1997) remarked that, "Historically, assessment of secondary trauma has been problematic because its effects are often less severe and consequently more difficult to detect than those due to primary trauma. Virtually all studies of secondary trauma have relied on paper and pencil measures or interviews and are subject to measurement and interpretation errors" (p. 896).

Currently, a measure of compassion fatigue and burnout among mental health workers is the only paper-and-pencil tool available. A literature search confirmed this assertion and existing assessment resources are described below.

EVALUATION RESOURCES

Assessment Questionnaires

Secondary Trauma Questionnaire

Stamm, B. (2002). Measuring compassion satisfaction as well as fatigue: Developmental history of the compassion satisfaction and fatigue test. In C. Figley (Ed.), *Treating compassion fatigue* (pp. 107–118). Philadelphia, PA: Brunner-Routledge.

Traumagram Questionnaire

Figley, C. (1989). *Helping traumatized families*. San Francisco: Jossey-Bass.

Scales

Secondary Traumatic Stress Scale (STSS)

Bride, B., Robinson, M., Yegidis, B., & Figley, C. (2003). Development and validation of the secondary traumatic stress scale. *Research on Social Work Practice, 13,* 1–16.

INFORMATION RESOURCES

Books

Figley, C. (Ed.). (1995). *Compassion fatigue: Coping with secondary traumatic stress disorder in those who treat the traumatized.* New York: Brunner/Mazel.
Figley, C. (Ed.). (2002). *Treating compassion fatigue.* Philadelphia, PA: Brunner/Routledge.
Stamm, B. (Ed.). (1995). *Secondary traumatic stress: Self-care issues for clinicians, researchers, and educators.* Towson, MD: Sidran Press.
Stamm, B. (Ed.). (1999). *Secondary traumatic stress: Self-care issues for clinicians, researchers, and educators* (2nd ed.). Towson, MD: Sidran Press.

Journals

Traumatology. URL: http://www.fsu.edu/~trauma.

Organizations

The Traumatology Institute. URL: http://www.cpd.fsu.edu/humanserv/trama.html.

6

Critical Incident Stress

Lydia was visibly upset during clinical rounds while describing a patient who was assessed the previous evening at an adult psychiatric clinic. The distraught patient reported swallowing an undisclosed amount of pills. During the physical examination, Lydia was alarmed when noticing that scars covered the patient's body. Although the presenting problem was not unusual, Lydia went on to report that the patient had an extensive record at the clinic and been seen over 50 times for similar behaviors.

During the meeting, Lydia was visibly troubled by the fact that the patient had such a long and unfortunate history of personal torment and self-mutilation. More troubling was the behavior of some staff who laughed and made snide and degrading remarks about the patient. In short, Lydia was shocked by two major events: the patient's condition and staff's response to the patient.

As she described the situation with other medical students and medical advisors, Lydia revealed her disorientation during the intake process. Lydia explained that although she was introduced to the problem of self-mutilation during medical school, the actual exposure to such a severe case of self-abuse was overwhelming. The effect of the event was obvious when she was unable to record her observations due to sweaty and trembling hands. Although Lydia was given the opportunity to debrief with the consulting psychiatrist, she felt nauseous and was unable to sleep. During her presentation, Lydia wondered how an individual could be so unhappy.

CONSTRUCT OVERVIEW

Critical incidents have been defined as "… specific, often unexpected, time-limited events that may involve loss or threat to personal goals or well-being, and may represent a potential turning point in the person's life" (Everly, Flannery, & Mitchell, 2000, p. 24). Critical events are outside the usual realm of human experience and are markedly distressing. Such events can evoke adverse psychological and physiological reactions, or both. As a result of the psychological trauma associated with significant critical events, normal coping mechanisms break down and negative health consequences can ensue (Flannery, 1999). This response can dramatically affect how professionals function at work, with their families, and socially.

Critical incident stress stems from a single event or a series of very traumatic events that overwhelm the helping professional's resources. Some of the significant events reported by helping professionals include: death of children, injury to children, death of any person, threatening events, knowing the victim, and grotesque sights and sounds exhibited by victims. To better articulate critical incident stress (CIS), the International Critical Incident Stress Foundation, Inc. (ICISF) identified *critical incident stress syndrome* as a milder reaction to a stressor and *critical incident stress disorder* as a severe reaction to a stress stimuli.

Critical Incident Stress Management versus Critical Incident Stress Debriefing

Critical incident stress management and critical incident stress are very important methods within the critical incident stress literature. As such, each method is described below and distinctions can be made.

Critical Incident Stress Management. Critical Incident Stress Management (CISM) was a departure from early crisis intervention models, represented a new model of intervention, and tailored intervention for differing needs. "CISM represents an integrated, comprehensive multicomponent crisis intervention program that spans the complete crisis continuum from the precrisis and acute crisis phases through the postcrisis phase" (Everly et al., 2000, p. 23). The purpose of CISM intervention is to (1) moderate the intense emotional distress that can accompany psychological crisis and mitigate acute stress disorder and (2) prevent or mitigate the onset of posttraumatic stress disorder (Crawford & Flannery, 2002).

As discussed hereunder, a range of crisis intervention services underpin CISM and include preincident phase, acute care interventions, and postincident response for victims. It should be mentioned that, depending on the source, these stages have been given different titles (e.g., precrisis preparedness training, individual crisis counseling, short group transitional/psycheducational interventions, short group decompression intervention, critical incident stress debriefing, family support intervention, and professional referrals).

TABLE 6.1
Critical Incident Stress Symptomatology

Emotional	Cognitive	Physical	Behavioral
Apprehensive	Confused	Chills	Withdrawal
Fearful	Nightmares	Thirst	Antisocial acts
Guilt	Uncertainty	Fatigue	Inability to rest
Grief	Hypervigilant	Nausea	Intensified pacing
Panic	Suspicious	Fainting	Erratic movements
Denial	Intrusive thoughts	Twitches	Change in social activities
Anxious	Blaming others	Vomiting	Change in speech patterns
Agitated	Poor problem solving	Dizziness	Loss/increase of appetite
Depressed	Inattentive	General weakness	Increased alcohol consumption
Intense anger	Poor decision-making	Chest pain	Change in usual communication
Emotional outbursts	Poor abstract thinking	Headaches	
Shocked	Poor concentration	Elevated blood pressure	
Overwhelmed	Poor memory	Rapid heart rate	
Out of control	Disorientation of time, place, or people	Muscle tremors, Grinding teeth	
Inappropriate responses	Increased/decreased awareness of surroundings	Shock	
Increased irritability		Visual difficulties	
Hypervigilant to environment		Profuse sweating	
		Difficulty breathing	

Source: Adapted from: http://www.icisf.com

Preincident Phase. The preincident phase involves establishing appropriate expectations for actual incident responses. More precisely, a focus is placed on enhancing the cognitive resources and coping skills of helping professionals.

Acute Care Intervention. Acute care intervention can include individual, family, or group services. Individual intervention can occur in a variety of settings (e.g., psychiatric emergency rooms, outpatient clinics, shelters, suicide prevention programs, and independent practice). Although not elaborating on specific individual-based counseling approaches, Everly, Flannery, and Mitchell (2000) pointed to empirical studies that support the clinical efficacy of individual crisis counseling.

According to Crawford and Flannery (2002), counselors are trained to provide emotional support, family crisis intervention, and grief counseling for families, or a combination of these things. Intervention generally includes up to three individual family sessions or six family group sessions.

Postincident Response. Postincident response can include additional medical, psychological, or social support services. To ensure adequate follow-up care, referrals are made to appropriate professionals when indicated.

Critical Incident Stress Debriefing

Critical incident stress debriefing (CISD) is a concept that originated in the military but is now used in health care organizations (Hollister, 1996). In reference to CISD, Hollister wrote:

> It began as a method for interrogators to get accurate information for a report. This objective was accomplished in a group setting, the premise being that a soldier was less likely to confuse the facts of an incident in the presence of peers because other soldiers would be able to corroborate his or her statement. (p. 44)

According to Richards (2001), CISD is "… defined as a meeting of those involved in a traumatic event which aims to diminish the impact of the event by promoting support and encouraging processing of traumatic experiences in a group setting. It attempts to accelerate recovery before harmful stress reactions have a chance to damage the performance, careers, health and families of victims" (p. 352). In providing some historical background regarding CISD, Hollister (1996) stated that in 1987 the Oregon Health Sciences University,

> … was one of the first hospitals in the United States to incorporate a debriefing team into its hospital personnel. The need for a home-based team was identified based on an increase of admissions, especially pediatric, and deaths that had occurred during their hospital stay. The administrative staff discovered the effect on employees was decreased job performance, satisfaction, and morale. (p. 47)

During the past two decades, three models of psychological debriefing have been developed and include Critical Incident Stress Debriefing (otherwise known as the Mitchell Model), the Raphael Model, and Process Debriefing.

The Seven Phases of Critical Incident Stress Debriefing

1. Introduction Phase During this phase, facilitators set ground rules such as initiating a therapeutic relationship and exploring issues of confidentiality.

2. Fact Phase During this phase, facilitators listen to clients describe their role in the event and provide factual accounts of what happened.

3. Thought Phase During this phase, facilitators encourage the client to put words to their first thought during the event.

4. Reaction Phase During this phase, facilitators enable clients to move from the cognitive level to the emotional level enabling clients to express the powerful emotions attached to their experience.

5. Symptom Phase During this phase, facilitators encourage clients to explore the thoughts, feelings, and behaviors they experienced during the event.

6. Teaching Phase During this phase, facilitators provide educational input about stress reactions and how to cope with them.

7. Reentry Phase During this phase, facilitators encourage clients to continue with counseling and provide a list of relevant resources available in their area.

Critical Incident Stress Debriefing Controversy

Despite its reputed importance and effectiveness, controversy regarding effectiveness and appropriateness hounds this method (e.g., Deahl, 2000; Galliano, 2002; Gist & Devilly, 2002; Gist & Woodall, 1998; Hiley-Young & Gerrity, 1994; Raphael & Ursano, 2002; Tobin, 2001). In discussing the status of psychological debriefing, Everly, Boyle, and Lating (1999) stated that, "It has been 15 years since psychological debriefing first appeared. Although widely practised, with numerous anectodal and case studies supporting its efficacy, psychological debriefings have only recently generated more systematic inquiries into their effectiveness" (p. 229). Irving and Long (2001) and Richards (2001) underscored the ongoing debate regarding the efficacy of CISD. Irving and Long elaborated,

> The literature on critical incident stress debriefing demonstrates that there are scholars and practitioners who support its use. There are others, however, who oppose it and still others who believe that it has a specific role and therefore work at identifying the *best possible* framework to ensure it is employed appropriately and to best effect. (p. 308).

It appears that the major concern regarding CISD relates to a lack of methodologically sound outcome research (Gist & Woodall, 1998). Furthermore, there is also some concern that CISD has the potential to create iatrogenic effects (Harris, Baloglu, & Stacks, 2002) or harm (Irving

& Long, 2001; Moran, 1998). This latter position has been supported by van Emmerik, Kamphuis, Hulsbosch, and Emmelkamp (2002) who charged: "Despite the intuitive appeal of the technique, our results show that CISD has no efficacy in reducing symptoms of posttraumatic stress disorder and other trauma-related symptoms, and in fact suggest that it has a detrimental effect" (p. 769). As with any good debate, Turnbull, Busuttil, and Pitman (1997) stirred the soup and argued that Bisson, Jenkins, Alexander, and Bannister (1997) misinterpreted the purpose of CISD and "... may unfairly influence clinicians not to practice psychological debriefing (PD)" (p. 582).

Deahl (2000) noted that "... numerous variations on the basic model of Mitchell have been developed" (p. 932). For example, Juhnke (1997) described how school counselors might use an adapted version of the CISD model to address student and parent needs following an incident of school violence. Irving and Long (2001) also modified the CISD model when working with three women who experienced traumatic life events.

AFFECTED POPULATIONS

As demonstrated below, critical incident stress has been reported within various helping professions and also within specialty areas (e.g., phychiatric nursing, child homicide investigation, ambulance service personnel).

Nurse Critical Incident Stress

Psychiatric Nursing. Based on a review of the literature, Antai-Otong (2001) asserted that psychiatric nurses are likely to experience workplace violence. According to Antai-Otong psychiatric nurses are usually exposed to verbally and physically abusive patients and reported, "Psychiatric nurses are more likely to encounter workplace violence than nurses in other settings and must prepare themselves using proactive healthpromoting activities; for example, the Critical Incident Stress Debriefing (CISD) model" (p. 125). In addition to contending with direct abusive behavior, these professionals must remain on guard in order to protect themselves and others.

As a result of this work environment, psychiatric nurses experience autonomic nervous system arousal and, thus, expend enormous energy and experience cumulative stress reactions.

To complicate matters, Antai-Otong (2001) noted that psychiatric nurses and management frequently minimize critical events and their traumatic experience. She wrote, "Part of this reaction or attitude

TABLE 6.2
Employee Reaction to Critical Incident Stress

Critical Episode	Reaction	Consequence
Robberies	Vulnerability Violation	Heightened suspicion Trepidation
Murder, bomb threat, vandalism, suicide	Dazed Shaken Incensed	Hypervigilance Anger Ambivalence
Employee Death from Illness	Disbelief Shock Regret	Anxiety
Corporate Downsizing	Shock Demoralization	Sense of Betrayal Anger Confusion Panic

involves socialization or cultural issues, particularly for men, who often feel it is socially unacceptable to cry, feel sad, be frightened, or grieve about an incident" (p. 130).

Advanced Practice Nursing. Sacks, Clements, and Fay-Hillier (2001) discussed the use of Critical Incident Stress Debriefing by advanced practice nurses. According to these authors, due to the increase in workplace violence, organizations are intervening to prevent, detect, and treat psychological posttrauma. Traumatic events ranging from bank and pharmacy robberies, murders, bomb threats, vandalism, to corporate downsizing can contribute to critical incident stress. As illustrated in Table 6.2., Sacks and colleagues (2001) provide poignant examples of how critical events can affect employees.

In providing these examples, the formidable task of advanced practice nurses who attempt to help clients through CISD is underlined. During the helping process, these professionals face "… a wide variety of employee and management reactions and emotions" (Sacks et al., 2001, p. 134).

Community Health Nursing. Hollister (1996) believed that Critical Incident Stress Debriefing could be useful for both health care professionals and victims since professionals frequently feel they could have been more helpful. As previously noted, events such as increased pediatric admissions and deaths during a hospital stay can contribute to critical incident stress.

Physician Critical Incident Stress

Medical Examiner. The medical examiner's office is considered an integral part of an emergency response team and vulnerable to critical incident stress. Crawford and Flannery (2002) noted that the medical examiners could be the first contact for family survivors. Consequently, professionals within this context are burdened with the responsibility of explaining the cause of death and arranging for the release of the remains. According to Crawford and Flannery (2002) due to the unique demands of their work, professionals within the medical examiner's office may experience psychological distress as a result of being continually exposed to stressful events. These authors also highlighted various cultural beliefs and practices professionals might have to consider while working with grieving families and relatives.

Police Officer Critical Incident Stress

Leonard and Alison (1999) contrasted two groups of police officers who were involved in shooting incidents. The purpose of the study was to explore appraisal and coping behaviors and the effect of the critical incident stress debriefing procedure. Results from this study demonstrated the problem with attributing change to any one intervention. These researchers concluded that, despite differences between the debriefed and nondebriefed groups in their response to shooting incidents, a myriad of factors must be considered. For example, previous involvement in negative life events, opposed to the shooting incident, may contribute to CIS symptomatology. In summary, Leonard and Alison (1999) affirmed:

> Whilst the results suggest that CISD may have had some impact as a crisis intervention strategy for reducing the effects of long-term stress symptoms, a direct test of its effectiveness was not possible because of the multitude of external factors that were a significant part of the officers' lives. (p. 158)

Child Homicide Investigator. Homicide investigators frequently investigate horrific crimes that sometimes involve children (Van Patten & Burke, 2001). Based on the experience of these authors, crimes involving children are the most difficult for investigators and such crimes can negatively influence the professional's emotional and psychological equilibrium. More specifically, Van Patten and Burke noted: "A child victim represents a unique case in that it is considerably more difficult for investigators to create the emotional distance necessary to protect themselves" (p. 136).

Public Service Personnel Critical Incident Stress

Public service personnel (firefighters, medical personnel, law enforcement personnel, and ambulance workers) can experience CIS symptomatology when victims are known. Jambois-Rankin (2000) wrote,

> Visualization was clearly the most prominent symptom noted by both groups. The physical and cognitive symptoms of stress reported increased with the emergence of much higher levels of grief being experienced by those personnel who had cared for victims who were known to them. (p. 85)

Based on her findings, she noted interesting areas for future investigation. For example, future research could explore the experiences of public service personnel who care for relatives. Differences in emotional responses between the genders can also be examined.

Firefighter Critical Incident Stress

Due to the nature of their work, firefighters are exposed to troubling sights, sounds, smells, and unfortunate memories. It has also been further suggested that the boundary between firefighters and the public has eroded and firefighters have become more exposed to emotionally distressed communities (Harris, Baloglu, & Stacks, 2002).

In an effort to determine if critical incident stress debriefing protected these professionals from stress-related disorders, Harris and colleagues (2002) conducted a study that examined the relationships between critical incident stress debriefings and various mental health variables in a large sample of firefighters. Based on their findings, these authors concluded, "… we find no evidence of a significant direct contribution to debriefing to coping skills or traumatic stress reactions" (p. 232). These authors further reported, "Our results are recommended to provide guidance with caution for future research and policy decisions regarding CISD and similar occupational interventions, and in particular to temper any overzealous claims regarding the efficacy and indications of CISD" (p. 234).

Ambulance Service Personnel Critical Incident Stress

Suserud, Blomquist, and Johansson (2002) discussed the exposure of ambulance workers to threats and violence. Moreover, these researchers described how the professional-patient relationship can be damaged and how professionals can experience an unexpected crisis. The authors argued:

Violence and threats can cause great damage to those who are its victims. Quite apart from fear, violence also means an infringement that affects one's self respect and integrity. It is the individual's experience of losing control and becoming vulnerable that is the important point, and not the incident itself. To be subjected to an act of violence, which comes suddenly and unexpectedly, can be most enervating even if the individual act is not serious. (p. 133)

It was interesting to learn that despite the acts of violence perpetrated against these professionals, many of these professionals experienced frustration because they were unable to provide patients with the required care. The issue of patient care, and more specifically the insufficient time to care for victims and their relatives, was previously raised (Suserud, 2001). McFarlane and Bookless (2001) appeared to encapsulate these findings when commenting, "It is a powerful and often altruistic motive for individuals to take on such roles as belonging to emergency service organizations to protect the well-being of society" (p. 261).

Funeral Director Critical Incident Stress

Kroshus and Swarthout (1995, para. 20) remarked:

The emotional cost borne by funeral directors as they prepare individuals for burial and guide bereaved families through the beginning process of grief is too often unrecognized. Their profession exacts a toll that is frequently manifested by a reduced ability to work and can become serious enough to cause a myriad of illnesses, interpersonal dysfunction, and ultimately death.

In order to further explore this area, these authors developed a questionnaire to "… investigate the relationship between exposures to critical incidents and the subsequent development of symptoms commonly associated with critical incident stress among funeral directors" (para. 5). This study also differentiated between urban and rural professionals. Results indicated that metropolitan funeral directors experienced frequent exposure to industrial accidents, explosions, boating accidents, sudden infant death syndrome deaths, airplane accidents, motorcycle fatalities, and homicides. Rural funeral directors, on the other hand, experienced frequent exposure to automobile accidents and farm accidents.

Results from this study showed that a very high percentage of respondents reported moderate to severe symptomatology. Moreover, directors in the 30- to 39-year-old age group were more likely to leave the funeral business. Although conceding that a cause-effect relationship cannot be made, the authors suggested that this particular age group may be more vulnerable to critical incident stress and may, therefore, benefit from preventative strategies.

Health Care Personnel Critical Incident Stress

Attention has been devoted to critical incident stress within the health care profession. More specifically, the potential impact of critical incident stress on health care providers, as well as health care organizations, has been highlighted. Spitzer and Burke (1993), for example, suggested that critical incident stress can present grave danger to patients, families, or other staff who expect professional competency and safe intervention. If the stress of the professional remains unattended, symptomatology can include cognitive impairments (e.g., diminished memory), emotional reactions (e.g., increased anger, fear, depression), and physical ailments (e.g., exhaustion, headaches) (Spitzer & Burke, 1993).

Unique programs designed to meet the emotional needs of health care professionals have been instituted. In response to a call from staff, LeBrocq, Charles, Chan, and Buchana (2003), for example, described the implementation of bereavement programs in hospital emergency departments. Emergency room staff expressed their frustration with the lack of help they were receiving when involved in the care of deceased patient and their families. In addition, these programs were implemented to circumvent any long-term negative effects on staff (e.g., unresolved grief, feelings of inadequacy).

INTERVENTION

As anticipated, the recommended intervention for critical incident stress involves critical incident stress management and critical incident stress debriefing. On a cautionary note, however, Moran (1998) highlighted individual differences and responses to traumatic events. In reference to emergency workers, she pointed out that ...debriefing may sometimes run counter to individual coping and impair rather than help some individuals" (para. 1).

SUMMARY

Although a range of symptoms has been associated with critical incident stress, a specific timeline has not been attached to this form of psychological injury. Perhaps the most important development materializing from the inception of this construct is the controversy surrounding critical incident stress debriefing. As noted earlier, the appropriateness of this intervention remains questionable.

Despite its popularity, only one evaluation questionnaire is available. Similarly, resource information regarding CIS is limited.

EVALUATION RESOURCES

Diagnostic Questionnaires

Critical Incident Stress Management Provider Questionnaire

Wee, D., & Myers, D. (2003). Compassion satisfaction, compassion fatigue, and critical incident stress management. *International Journal of Emergency Mental Health, 5,* 33–37.

INFORMATION RESOURCES

Books

Lewis, G. (1994). *Critical incident stress and trauma in the workplace.* Bristol, PA: Accelerated Development.

Mitchell, J., & Everly, G. (2001). *Critical incident stress debriefing: An operation manual for CISD, defusing, and other group crisis intervention services.* Ellicott, MD: Chevron.

Organizations

International Critical Incident Stress Foundation, Inc. URL: http://www.icisf.org.

7

Vicarious Traumatization

Debbie's wish to practice her clinical social work skills came to fruition when given the opportunity to work directly with women who were victims of spousal abuse. Her clinical experience included performing psychosocial assessments, providing supportive counseling, and arranging group counseling participation. At first, Debbie was thrilled with the prospect of helping women to understand patterns of abuse while revisioning their future. During her first few weeks, Debbie received many compliments from the clients and staff for her insight and natural ability to empathize.

Although Debbie was gaining invaluable experience and knowledge regarding the problem of domestic violence, she was beginning to question the quality of her own intimate relationship. After hearing about horrific stories of abuse, and seeing the physical results of brutality, Debbie slowly began to question whether she was being exploited and a potential victim of abuse. Rather than returning home to prepare for an evening's activity with her partner Linda, Debbie was increasingly vigilant around personal space and boundaries. Although trying to appreciate the demands associated with Debbie's learning experience, Linda voiced her concerns about the emotional distance that had developed between them. From her perspective, there had been a major change in their relationship since Debbie embarked on her clinical experience. In her opinion, Debbie had become emotionally distant and protective of her physical space.

During group supervision, Debbie alluded to the fact that women in general should remain hypervigilant in their relationships to avoid exploitation and abuse. She further remarked that prior to her clinical experience she was very naïve and vulnerable. As the supervisor queried Debbie, it became evident that she was being greatly influenced by the emotional and physical condition of her clients and their horrific stories of abuse. In response, Debbie was struggling with trust and intimacy, had become suspicious of people, and was developing a self-protective shield.

CONSTRUCT OVERVIEW

Vicarious traumatization has been defined as "... the transformation in the inner experience of the therapist that comes about as a result of the empathic engagement with clients' trauma material" (Pearlman & Saakvitne, 1995, p. 31). These authors asserted that the effects of vicarious traumatization were widespread and its costs were immeasurable. In their opinion, the experience of vicarious traumatization inevitably affects professional and personal relationships. According to Pearlman and Saakvitne (1995) this material can include: graphic descriptions of violent events, exposure to the realities of people's cruelty to one another, and involvement in or witnessing traumatic events.

Sabin-Farrell and Turpin (2003) provided a comprehensive review of the extant literature and research regarding vicarious traumatization and call into question the validity and need for this construct. More specifically, these authors charged, "Even if the existence of VT [vicarious traumatization] can be established, the question remains whether we need a new construct to describe these various symptoms of distress arising from involvement in trauma work" (p. 452).

TABLE 7.1
Vicarious Traumatization Symptomatology

Emotional	Cognitive	Physical	Behavioral
Less grounded	Feeling unworthy of love	Feeling unsafe	Social withdrawal
Overwhelmed	Feeling unloved	Intrusive visual, auditory, sensory, and olfactory imagery	Disconnected from loved ones
Frustrated	Question right to be alive/happy		Crying episodes
Unbearably anxious	Self- loathing		Eruptions of anger
Unable to experience pleasure	Poor decision- making		Intolerant
Emotionally numb	Feeling like a failure		Distant from others
Emotionally closed	Lack of trust		Harsh
Despair	Cynical		Disconnection from significant others
Resentful	Intrusive imagery		Poor judgment
Exhausted			Loss of control
Flooding reminders			Nightmares
			Avoidance of of traumatic event

Adapted from Saakvitne, K., & Pearlman, L. (1996). *Transforming the pain: A workbook on vicarious traumatization for helping professionals who work with traumatized clients.* New York: Norton.

AFFECTED POPULATIONS

As demonstrated below, vicarious traumatization has been reported within various helping professions and also within specialty areas (e.g., sexual assault counselling, emergency room nursing, medical social work).

Counselor Vicarious Traumatization

Trauma Counseling. Sexton (1999) reviewed the literature regarding the effect of trauma on counselors. He found that most of the literature was based on anecdotal experiences and systematic research was scant.

In his review, Sexton addressed the issue of vicarious traumatization on organizations and suggested the suffering of traumatized counselors can potentially impact their place of employment.

A study by Black and Weinreich (2001) supported this earlier claim. These authors conducted a study to determine the ways that counselors construct their identity when exposed to client trauma. Results showed that vicarious traumatization can have a prolonged and negative impact on counselor identity. Along with a call for more research, Black and Weinreich (2001) encouraged the caring professions to heighten awareness regarding the effects of vicarious traumatization on counselors who deal with trauma.

Although in reference to the interview process, and not counseling per se, Goldenberg (2002) explored the experiences of individuals who interviewed Holocaust survivors. This small exploratory study suggested more positive impacts than negative impacts. For example, researchers gained an increased appreciation for survivor resilience and strength and a greater appreciation for their own lives.

Sexual Assault Counseling. The need to protect counselors who work with survivors of childhood sexual abuse was emphasized by Etherington (2000). Various unconscious dynamics that can contribute to vicarious traumatization are discussed and include countertransference, identification with victims, identification with the role of rescuer, and identification with the abuser.

The vicarious traumatization of women psychotherapists who provide services to sexual abuse survivors has been explored (Brady, Guy, Poelstra, & Brokaw, 1999). These authors posed important questions regarding the influence and potential harm of trauma work on psychologists. Through their study, it was determined that female psychotherapists who work with survivors may experience mild intrusion and avoidance symptoms. Moreover, long-term effects on cognitive schemas and beliefs were unlikely to result. It was concluded that, "Female clinicians appear to be fairly hardy, having world views and perceptions of self and persons in their environment that do not differ from their colleagues" (p. 391).

Schauben and Frazier (1995) noted a scarcity of research regarding how counselors are influenced by their work with victims of sexual violence. To begin filling this void, these authors embarked on a study to investigate how female counselors are affected by their work with victims. Results from their study showed that counselors who worked with a high percentage of survivors reported more disrupted beliefs about self and others, more posttraumatic stress disorder–related symptoms, and more vicarious trauma. An important finding from this study was that counselors with a personal history of sexual abuse were no more distressed when doing trauma work than counselors who did not have a history of victimization.

In their qualitative study involving 12 female psychologists and counselors, Steed and Downing (1998) found that these helping professionals experienced a variety of severe negative effects when working with victims of sexual abuse and assault. Negative effects reported by participants included a sense of increased vulnerability, increased self-protective strategies, heightened suspicion and mistrust, and disruptions to cognitive schemas. These findings supported Johnson and Hunter's (1997) earlier conclusions that sexual assault counselors experienced more stress in their work than did other counselors.

Domestic Violence Counseling. Iliffe and Steed (2000) remarked that counselors who work with victims of trauma may been hidden victims themselves. These authors reported that there was little research regarding counselors who work with domestic violence. To explore this area, Iliffe and Steed (2000) conducted a qualitative study involving 18 counselors. The authors extracted major themes from the interviews that included (1) initial impact of domestic violence counseling, (2) personal impact of hearing traumatic material, (3) changes to cognitive schemas, and (4) challenging issues. It was concluded that many of the phenomena associated with vicarious traumatization were reported by study participants.

Nurse Vicarious Traumatization

Emergency Room Nursing. Little (2002) reported that, "… emergency nurses also witness cruel and, at times, malicious acts of inhumanity toward others, acts which often result in human suffering" (p. 27). In describing the work environment of emergency nurses, Little discussed the intense emotional state of nurses and how this emotional state is intensified when these professionals are unable to alleviate patient suffering.

Childhood Trauma Nurse Vicarious Traumatization. The challenge in working with survivors of childhood trauma can be enormous (Crothers, 1995; Blair & Ramones, 1996). Crothers elaborated on her interviews with nurses and discussed the potential systemic impact of this work (e.g., work setting, family, leisure time). Furthermore, she mentioned that the task of nurses involved a willingness to hear the past experiences of patients, help patients remain based in day-to-day living, and remain cognizant of patient strengths and resources. This is no easy feat when considering the psychiatric problems of patients and the need to protect oneself from the contagion effect of trauma through the establishment of appropriate boundaries.

Disaster Nursing. Miller (1992) revealed that despite learning to deal with tragic situations (e.g., patient death), "Nurses frequently berate themselves for reacting to crisis with strong emotion" (p. 58). She further remarked that these professionals need to be reminded that the situation is abnormal and not their reaction. Familiar smells, sounds, and media reports can influence nurse reactions.

Therapist Vicarious Traumatization

Therapists who work with trauma victims could experience an alternation or disruption in their cognitive schemas and imagery system of memory as a result of exposure to client victimization (McCann & Pearlman, 1990). According to these authors, these changes may be subtle or shocking and will depend upon "… the degree of discrepancy between the client's traumatic memories and the therapist's existing schemas" (p. 138). McCann and Pearlman list several schemas that can be affected (e.g., dependency/trust, safety, power, intimacy).

Neumann and Gamble (1995) reported that therapists who work with trauma survivors frequently experience posttraumatic sequela similar to clients. In terms of new therapists, these authors remarked: "New therapists exposed to the graphic material of trauma clients may be dismayed and surprised to find themselves becoming more suspicious of others, increasingly worried about personal safety, despairing about the violence and cruelty in our society, and pessimistic about the power of psychotherapy to make a difference" (p. 344). Several factors that might contribute to new therapist vulnerability were identified and included: (1) lack of collegial and technical support due to their position at the bottom of an organizational hierarchy, (2) being asked to work with very difficult cases, (3) believing that professionals are inoculated from the effects of human suffering, performance anxiety, and (4) lack of role modeling.

Social Worker Vicarious Traumatization

Medical Social Work. A pilot study was conducted to determine whether social workers working in medical settings were vulnerable to vicarious trauma (Dane & Chachkes, 2001). Although findings from this study identified the major themes of organizational stress, guilt, and problems in coping with the emotional impact of cases, it was concluded that the work experiences of participants did not provoke emotional disturbances that eventuated in vicarious traumatization.

Child Protection Work. Horwitz (1998) argued, "Social worker trauma can occur when a caseload event or series of events is beyond the capacity of the social worker to manage" (p. 365). The author also described the direct and indirect trauma social workers could experience when working in child protection. Direct trauma included assaults and vandalism, threats of assaults, public sources (e.g., harassment, criticism), and organizational demands. Indirect trauma included exposure to dismal events or emotional contagion. When outlining the potential effects of trauma, Horwitz alluded to worker vulnerability and past life events.

INTERVENTION

From the outset, it should be noted that Saakvitne and Pearlman (1996) have written a workbook specific to helping professional vicarious traumatization. This workbook, combined with the additional interventions that follow, provides helping professionals with a wide variety of intervention strategies.

Debriefing

Individual (Goldenberg, 2002) and group psychological debriefings (Everly, Boyle, & Lating 1999; Miller, 1992) are common practices to mitigate vicarious traumatization. In summarizing the group approach, Everly and colleagues (1999) stated:

> The debriefing technology is a structured group discussion of a crisis or traumatic event wherein participants are encouraged to discuss their respective cognitive perceptions of, as well as affective and physical reactions to, a crisis or traumatic event. In addition to verbal representations and cathartic ventilation, debriefings represent an early intervention forum wherein patholytic factors of group support, normalization (demedicalization), health education, stress management and assessment for follow-up/referral are harnessed within a 1–3 hour crisis intervention protocol. (p. 230)

According to Miller (1992) relief may result from a debriefing support group when thoughts and feelings related to a trauma are shared.

Training/Supervision

Brady and colleagues (1999) noted the value of clinical training and practice programs for students who are interested in working with trauma survivors. Pearlman and MacIan (1995) also highlighted the need for training in trauma therapy for novice therapists and more supervision by seasoned trauma therapists. Other authors (Crothers, 1995; Etherington, 2000) have elaborated on the use of supervisory support to assist helping professionals avoid or alleviate vicarious trauma. Crothers (1995) and Sexton (1999) have noted the potential benefits of both individual and group supervision. More specifically, the need for counselor understanding, reframing, and boundary setting has been emphasized (Crothers, 1995; Sexton, 1999).

Staff Support/Development

The value of informal support networks and staff development programming has not gone unnoticed (Black & Weinreich, 2001; Crothers, 1995; Goldenberg, 2002; Ruzek, 1993; Schauben & Frasier, 1995). Ruzek (1993, para. 7) commented: "Therapists who work with traumatized people require an ongoing support system to deal with these intense reactions. Just as no survivor can recover alone, no therapist can work with trauma alone."

Mental Health Days

Crothers (1995) suggested utilizing accrued sick leave and mental health days to revitalize and care for oneself. Perhaps during these time periods, helping professionals can reflect on the need to maintain realistic expectations (McCann & Pearlman, 1990). Schauben and Frasier (1995) commented that helping professionals also participate in meditation and cognitive restructuring.

Personal Life

Enjoying activities outside of work and a fulfilling personal life have been recommended (Crothers, 1995; Sexton, 1999). Saakvitne (1995) wrote, "It is vital for a therapist in her personal life to think about and address many aspects of herself, not solely her caretaking functions and capacities or her analytic work" (p. 490). The importance of rest, exercise, nutrition, relaxation, and spirituality has also been addressed (Saakvitne, 1995; Sexton, 1999).

Balanced Workload

Iliffe and Steed (2000) found that helping professionals used various adaptive strategies to ensure their well-being. For example, strategies included the monitoring of client caseloads, debriefing, peer support, and self-care. Along with monitoring caseloads, McCann and Pearlman (1990) suggested adding variety to one's workload through the involvement of research and teaching. These authors also mentioned mixing client cases to create variety.

SUMMARY

Similar to critical incident stress, vicarious traumatization is accompanied by a wide range of symptoms but lacks a specific timeline. Information regarding evaluation resources is limited to one scale and one inventory.

Intervention appears to focus on providing support for helping professionals who are privy to tragic client stories. The use of debriefing and the value of staff development are also common forms of intervention. Finally, the need to prepare prospective professionals for the harsh realities of trauma work has also been recognized. Additional information regarding vicarious traumatization can be obtained through books and an organization, listed below.

EVALUATION RESOURCES

Inventories

Traumatic Stress Institute Life Orientation Inventory. URL: http://www.tsicaap.com.

Scales

Traumatic Stress Institute Belief Scale

Adams Betts, K., Matto, H., & Harrington, D. (2001). The Traumatic Stress Institute Belief Scale as a measure of vicarious trauma in a national sample of clinical social workers. *Families in Society: The Journal of Contemporary Human Services, 82,* 363–371.

INFORMATION RESOURCES

Books

McCann, L., & Pearlman, L. (1990). *Psychological trauma and the adult survivor.* New York: Brunner/Mazel.

Pearlman, L., & Saakvitne, K. (1995). *Trauma and the therapist: Countertransference and vicarious traumatization in psychotherapy with incest survivors.* New York: Norton.

Saakvitne, K. & Pearlman, L. (1996). *Transforming the pain: A workbook on vicarious traumatization for helping professionals who work with traumatized clients.* New York: Norton.

Organizations

Traumatic Stress Institute. URL: http://www.tsicaap.com.

8

Burnout

As director of the Marriage and Family Therapy Training program, Sam was considered an upbeat and enthusiastic individual who actively participated in group discussions and social functions. Over time, however, Sam appeared tired and irritable. His friendly smile disappeared and he became moody and temperamental. When a concerned colleague gently questioned Sam about this obvious behavior change, Sam became defensive and abruptly remarked, "People should worry about themselves." In addition to withdrawing from collegial conversations, Sam would sardonically dismiss students who questioned his agitated behavior.

Concern for Sam heightened when it was discovered that he was arriving late for clinical supervision duties and was leaving early on several occasions. Colleagues and students reported that Sam appeared lethargic and showed minimal initiative. During the midsemester review that included Sam, his colleagues, and the faculty dean, Sam revealed that he was unsure about his interest in marriage and family therapy practice and training. He reported feeling physically and emotionally exhausted, discouraged by minimal client progress, and indifferent about the need to help students develop their clinical skills. When queried further, he expressed his boredom and viewed his teaching and administrative tasks as mundane and meaningless.

CONSTRUCT OVERVIEW

There appears to be a general consensus throughout the literature that Freudenberger selected the term burnout to describe the emotional and physical exhaustion displayed by helping professionals. Burnout has been reviewed extensively in the literature (e.g., Farber, 1983; Freudenberger, 1974; Grosch & Olsen, 1994; Pines, 1993; Maslach, 1982). Pines and Aronson (1988) defined burnout as "... a state of physical, emotional and mental exhaustion caused by long term involvement in emotionally demanding situations" (p. 9). Other authors (Grosch & Olsen, 1994) perceived burnout as degenerative process, an erosion of spirit, and a loss of faith in the very enterprise of helping.

Professional helpers who are experiencing burnout report an extreme dissatisfaction with their clinical experience. This construct is characterized by excessive distancing from patients, impaired competence, low energy, increased irritability with supporters, and other signs of impairment and depression resulting from individual, social, and work environment, and social factors (Figley, 1995). According to Figley (1995) burnout is a process rather than a fixed condition that begins gradually and becomes progressively worse. The process includes (1) a gradual exposure to job strain, (2) erosion of idealism, and (3) a void of achievement. Grosch and Olsen (1994) suggested that helping professionals often do not recognize the problem of burnout until it has reached an advanced stage.

TABLE 8.1
Burnout Symptomatology

Emotional	Cognitive	Physical	Behavioral
Depression	Cynicism	Flare- ups of preexisting medical disorders	Increased consumption of caffeine, tabacco, alcohol, over- the- counter medications and prescription and illicit drugs
Hopelessness	Negativity	Headaches	High- risk behaviors
Helplessness	Sense of isolation	Physical depletion	Increased interpersonal conflicts
Anger	Sense of failure	Chronic fatigue	Tardiness
Disillusionment	Feeling trapped	Loss of vitality	Distrust
Frustration		Insomnia	
		Frequent and prolonged colds	
		Nightmares	
		Excessive Sleeping	
		Ulcers	
		Gastrointestinal disorders	
		Sudden weight gain or loss	
		Muscular Pain	
		Increased premenstrual syndrome	

Adapted from Pines, A. (1993). Burnout. In L. Goldberger and S. Breznitz (Eds.), *Handbook of Stress: Theoretical and Clinical Aspects* (2nd ed.). New York: Free Press.

AFFECTED POPULATIONS

As demonstrated below, burnout has been reported within various help-ing professions and also within specialty areas (e.g., HIV counseling, mental health nursing, psychistry and child psychiatry, geriatic social work).

Counselor Burnout

Career Counseling. Skovholt, Grier, and Hanson (2001) remarked: "The process of caring is made up of a constant series of empathic attachments, active involvements, and felt separations. The ability to continually engage in *the caring cycle* is important for success. However, the constant need to re-create the cycle of caring can lead to counselor depletion and burnout" (p. 167).

To contribute to career counselor well-being and longevity, these authors proposed a developmental framework. In doing so, they pre-sented a valuable list of occupational hazards to consider. Distinctions are also made regarding the demands experienced by novice versus experienced counselors. For example, novice counselors may feel inade-quate and unprepared whereas experienced counselors contend with issues that challenge their competency, client resistance or apathy, and so forth.

Child Maltreatment Counseling. Results from a study conducted by Stevens and Higgins (2002) suggested that counselors who work with maltreated children experienced high levels of emotional exhaustion and deperson-alization and a low to moderate sense of personal accomplishment.

HIV Counseling. Shoptaw, Stein, and Rawson (2000) stated:

> Working with HIV-infected clients often elicits from counselors feelings of depression, frustration, and helplessness that can result from the accep-tance of possessing limited abilities to mediate the client's suffering due to powerful influences, such as expensive medical care, limited affordable housing, and family problems. (p. 117)

These authors conducted a mail survey of 134 counselors and discovered that increased job support from colleagues and supervisors, and increased feelings of job efficacy generated less burnout. An interesting finding was that working in a methadone clinic was a risk factor for burnout. Factors that contribute to worker burnout included larger case-loads and the lack of opportunity to provide psychosocial support or services to clients.

Nurse Burnout

Hospital-Based Nursing. Buunk, Ybema, Van Der Zee, Schaufeli, and Gibbons (2001) claimed burnout was prevalent among nurses. This claim was supported by Aiken, Clarke, Sloane, Sochalski, and Silber (2002) who provided staggering statistics and sobering facts regarding hospital nurse burnout. These authors stated:

> Forty percent of hospital nurses have burnout levels that exceed the norms of health care workers. Job dissatisfaction among hospital nurses is 4 times greater than the average for all US workers, and 1 in 5 hospital nurses report that they intend to leave their current jobs within a year. (p. 1987)

Based on their comprehensive study of 168 hospitals, Aiken, Clarke, Sloane, Sochalski, and Silber (2002) concluded that high nurse-patient ratios were associated with burnout. Balevre (2001) explored the connection between burnout and irrational thinking and asserted: "Nurses who demand perfection and control in themselves and others create unrealistic demands and expectations that cannot be met in the real world of nursing" (p. 264). Nurses who persist in this thinking can experience frustration, stress, and burnout. Results from a study conducted by Sims (2001) revealed that nurse hardiness and spiritual well-being were related to lower levels of burnout.

Garrett and McDaniel (2001) investigated the correlation between environmental uncertainty and burnout. It was discovered that perceived environmental uncertainty could contribute to nurse burnout. Two important points emerged from the data. First, there was an increase in nurse emotional exhaustion and depersonalization when supervisor support was perceived as lacking. Second, there was an association between a perceived lack of peer cohesion and depersonalization.

The correspondence of hospital patient satisfaction and nurse burnout was explored by Leiter, Harvie, and Frizzell (1998). To no surprise, patients expressed satisfaction with services in contexts where nurses found their work meaningful. The opposite was also true. In other words, patients reported less satisfaction on units where nurses felt more exhausted and more frequently expressed an intention to quit. Results from this study point out how the emotional disposition of nurses can influence patients and their perceptions of care.

Mental Health Nursing. Tilley and Chambers (2003) noted the availability of information regarding mental health nursing supervision. They also reported on an ongoing investigation regarding the relationship between clinical supervision and burnout among mental health nurses. Preliminary findings indicated a low response rate, thus suggesting that mental health nursing could be an overresearched population.

Psychiatric Nursing. There is limited research regarding burnout among psychiatric nurses (Happell, Martin, & Pinikahana, 2003). To begin filling this void, these authors conducted a comparative study of psychiatric nurses from forensic and a mainstream mental health service. Findings indicated that nurses working in mainstream mental health service showed a higher level of burnout when compared to forensic nurses. Moreover, forensic psychiatric nurses recorded higher levels of job satisfaction. Specific areas of satisfaction for forensic nurses included their current work situation, involvement in decision-making, and support. In summary, Happell and colleagues wrote, ". . . the forensic psychiatric nurses are *less* burned out and *more* satisfied, whereas the mainstreamed psychiatric nurses are *more* burned out and *less* satisfied with their profession, work environment, peer support, and professional growth" (p. 46). Because these results appear contrary to popular belief, the need for further investigation as to why the forensic working environment appears more positive and supportive is warranted.

Physician Burnout

Spickard, Gabbe, and Christensen (2002) provided an excellent review of the literature regarding burnout in generalist and specialist physicians. It was the opinion of these authors that physician wellness is the responsibility of both the professional and the health care system. They further asserted: "Physicians must be guided from the earliest years of training to cultivate methods of personal renewal, emotional self-awareness, connection with social support systems, and a sense of mastery and meaning in their work" (p. 1450).

While describing their study regarding physician burnout, Graham, Potts, and Ramirez (2002) made obvious the conflicted findings in this area. In their study, these authors found an association between job stress and emotional exhaustion and psychiatric morbidity. They also noted that physicians who reported high levels of job satisfaction had better mental health.

Zaslove (2001) described a scenario that can culminate in physician burnout. Excessive patient demands and time restraints are underscored. Gundersen (2001) provided an excellent review of the extant literature regarding physician well-being and stated: "Physicians are often prone to burnout because of their personality profiles" (p. 145). She went on to say that physicians are generally driven, competitive, and like to excel. Furthermore, because physicians are discouraged from feeling too much sympathy or sadness, they close down emotionally. This perspective resounded a statement by Lake (cited in Hope, 2000), who described a depletion syndrome wherein physicians push themselves too hard for extended periods of time until their inner resources are depleted. A challenge in investigating physician burnout was underscored by Hope (2000), who claimed that physicians are often unwilling to admit to self or others that they have problems and reported that statistics regarding the pervasiveness of physician burnout were poor.

Psychiatry and Child Psychiatry. According to Korkeila, Toyry, Kumpulainen, Toivola, Rasanen, and Kalimo (2003) burnout and threat of severe burnout was more commonly reported by psychiatrists and child psychiatrists than other physicians. The symptoms of emotional exhaustion were most common among psychiatrists working in community care and child psychiatry contexts. Based on their results, the lack of consultation and supervision opportunities increased the likelihood of burnout.

Anesthesiology. When compared to their North American colleagues, Australian anesthetists showed identical scores for personal achievement but lower scores for emotional exhaustion and depersonalization. Despite subjective impressions, these Australian specialists did not appear to be at risk for burnout and job satisfaction appeared to be a protective factor against burnout (Kluger, Townend, & Laidlaw, 2003).

Family Physician Residency. Ospina-Kammerer and Figley (2003) underlined the scarcity of research regarding stress reduction of family physician residents and asserted: "Investigating family physician stress is important not only for the individual physician's well-being and patient care, but also for curriculum development and implementation of prevention and treatment programs" (p. 29).

To begin filling this void, Ospina-Kammerer and Figley (2003) evaluated the effectiveness of the Respiratory One Method (ROM) in reducing emotional exhaustion among family physician residents. Results from this study indicated that the ROM treatment did have an effect on emotional exhaustion subscale scores of the Maslach Burnout Inventory. Based on this preliminary study, family physicians were encouraged to remain cognizant of their personal health practices.

Police Officer Burnout

Research results obtained by Hawkins (2001) indicated that more than one-third of participants scored high in the area of emotional exhaustion and 56.1 percent scored high in the area of depersonalization. Additional profile data indicated that married officers appeared more prone to emotional exhaustion, officers who spent longer periods of time on a particular job were prone to emotional exhaustion, and the longer an officer was in law enforcement the greater probability that he or she would become emotionally exhausted.

Correctional Officer Burnout

Morgan, Van Haveren, and Pearson (2002) set out to clarify previous study results and expand research regarding correctional officer burnout. Based on the results of their research, ". . . older and more educated officers reported increased levels of personal accomplishment, whereas less experienced officers, and officers with increasing job responsibilities experienced increased levels of depersonalization and emotional exhaustion and decreased levels of personal accomplishment" (p. 144). These researchers also discovered that when compared to their male counterparts, female officers were less likely to". . . respond to inmates in an impersonal manner or with a lack of concern" (p. 153).

Psychologist Burnout

Licensed Psychology. In an early study, Ackerly, Burnell, Holder, and Kurdek (1988) used the surveyed 562 licensed, doctoral level, practicing psychologists who were primarily employed in human service settings throughout the United States. The Maslach Burnout Inventory was used to assess the extent of burnout. Findings illustrated that 39.9 percent of the surveyed psychologists experienced elevated levels of emotional exhaustion and 34.3 percent were experiencing elevated levels of depersonalization. Only 0.9 percent of psychologists experienced high reduced personal accomplishment. Results from the survey also revealed that 21.0 percent of surveyed psychologists would have chosen an alternate career path.

School Psychology. Following a comprehensive review of the literature, Huebner (1993) reported that research pertaining to burnout among school psychologists was meager and that the consequences of burnout could be serious for both school psychologists and recipients of care. He further noted that despite being perceived as a form of popular psychology, there was considerable research support for its construct validity, meaningfulness, and importance.

Huebner (1993) extracted three major factors regarding school psychologist burnout, which included organizational, interpersonal, and intrapersonal. Each factor was further broken down into different variables. For example, under the organizational factor important variables included structure, climate, role issues, and resources. It was concluded that additional research was necessary to explore school psychologist burnout and the impact of this disposition on recipient's care.

Research regarding job satisfaction, burnout, and perceived effectiveness was conducted by Proctor and Steadman (2003). Results from this small study indicated that psychologists who serve one school, versus those who serve multiple schools, enjoy higher rates of job satisfaction, lower rates of burnout, and perceive themselves as more effective.

Therapist Burnout

McCarthy and Frieze (1999) remarked that, "Burned-out therapists may exhibit certain behaviors that cause the client to feel that the quality of care he or she is receiving is substandard" (p. 34). These authors considered the relationship between feelings of therapist ineffectiveness, worthlessness, and burnout and eventual maladaptive clinical strategies and suspect client care. The inherent reciprocation of the therapeutic relationship alluded to by McCarthy and Frieze was addressed in a later study (Linehan, Cochran, Mar, Levensky, & Comtois, 2000). Linehan and colleagues discovered a therapist's high expectancy for therapeutic success could contribute to burnout. These authors elaborated,

> It may be that higher expectations lead to more therapeutic work which, in turn, leads to greater exhaustion. Or, it may be that therapists with high expectations are more likely to be disappointed in the rate of positive outcomes with BPD clients and that this disappointment, in turn, leads to demoralization and emotional exhaustion over time (p. 336).

This finding supports an earlier claim made by Williams (1989) who suggested that personal accomplishment may be integral in mediating the progression of burnout. Williams (1989) implied that emotional exhaustion could be tolerated if personal accomplishment remained high.

In their study. McCarthy and Frieze hypothesized that as a result of burnout, therapists used particular social influence strategies that impacted the quality of client care. These strategies included personal coercion, personal reward, compromise, and expert influence.

Social Worker Burnout

Clinical Social Work. Um and Harrison (1998) surveyed 165 clinical social workers in a quest to explore the relationship between job satisfaction and burnout. Results from this study indicated role conflict did intensify worker burnout. However, a strong relationship did not exist between burnout and job satisfaction, thus contradicting previous research.

General Practice Social Work. Soderfeldt, Soderfeldt, and Warg (1995) provided a comprehensive literature review regarding burnout within the social work profession. More specifically, they extracted various factors believed to contribute to social worker burnout. Following their review of the extant research, these authors asserted it was impossible to generalize to social workers as a group and concluded, "There should be an end to fishing expeditions based on the preconceptions that social workers are burned out. Instead, generalized studies with proper methodology should be carried out" (p. 645).

Koeske and Kelly (1995) surveyed 404 social workers from southwest Pennsylvania. The questionnaire included sections that queried participants about emotional exhaustion, involvement, job satisfaction, and social support. It was concluded from the results that overinvolved social workers exhibit an erosion of job satisfaction as a result of strain.

Geriatric Social Work. A longitudinal study that investigated burnout among social workers who work with elderly clients indicated that burnout was a relatively stable phenomenon (Poulin & Walker, 1993). This study suggested that low and high burnout among social workers was associated with organizational, client, and personal factors. It was interesting to learn that high burnout was reported by workers who experienced increased job stress, less organization and supervisor support, less satisfaction with clients, lower self-esteem, and increased hours worked per week.

Carrilio and Eisenberg (1984) examined a 3-year demonstration project that explored the relationship between social worker morale and mode of service delivery. These authors focused their attention on social workers who worked with an older and aging population. According to these authors the challenges faced by these helping professionals included confronting their own mortality, the deteriorating course of clients, and the vulnerability of their own parents. In short, it was suggested that given these factors, unresolved worker countertransference required attention to ensure the emotional well-being of these professionals.

Geriatric Caregiving. Little is known about stress and burnout levels in staff caregivers working within the geriatric field. A study by Cocco, Gatti, Lima, and Camus (2002) compared staff caregivers in acute geriatric wards of general hospitals to staff caregivers employed in nursing homes. Results from this study showed that ". . . levels of stress and burnout among staff caregivers are moderate in acute geriatric wards, but significantly higher than in nursing homes" (p. 78). Cocco and colleagues surmised that staff caregivers in general hospitals were less comfortable in the management of patients who exhibited psychiatric disorders, especially patients who displayed behavioral symptoms and personality change.

Helping Professional Burnout

Gabassi, Cervai, Rozbowsky, Semeraro, and Gregori (2002) compared volunteers and professionals and discovered that volunteers reported less emotional exhaustion when compared to professionals. In addition, volunteers seemed less cynical and enjoyed better relationships with consumers.

Clarkson (1992) examined the correlation between scripts and life positions, Freudenberger's typologies, and the transactional analysis concepts of the racket system. Clarkson discussed how nonproductive or destructive scripts that are assumed by helping professionals could contribute to burnout.

Working with Developmental Disabilities. Alexander and Hegarty (2000) conducted a study that involved using the Maslach Burnout Inventory to measure burnout among helping professionals who support people with learning disabilities. It should be noted that these authors provided an excellent overview regarding burnout among staff who worked with individuals presenting with emotional and developmental challenges, or both. The aforementioned study involved 13 staff members who were separated into 2 groups. Group 1 consisted of 6 day care staff and Group 2 consisted of 7 senior managers.

Results from this study indicated that staff in general experienced some level of burnout. Moreover, participants experienced moderate levels of emotional exhaustion, depersonalization, and reduced personal accomplishment. Interestingly, this study found: "The results do not show, as Maslach and Jackson originally suggested, that day care staff experience higher levels of burnout than senior staff. Rather it is the senior staff who are expressing higher emotional exhaustion and depersonalisation than the junior staff. There is no significant difference between the groups on personal accomplishment" (Alexander & Hegarty, 2000, p. 58). It was determined that day care staff and management personnel hold different views regarding the greatest demands of their work.

Working with Sex Offenders. Thorpe, Righthand, and Kubik (2001) contended: "Professionals working with convicted sex offenders or sex crime defendants encounter negative experiences that create the potential for professional burnout" (p. 198). To gauge the level of such negative experiences, these authors surveyed a variety of conference attendees (e.g., social workers, psychiatrists, judges) to investigate burnout. Results showed expected patterns. For instance, professionals who reported a heightened negative emotional impact of their work also reported more harmful impact on their professional performance. Further, participants who were successful in coping with work-related stress experienced less damaging impact on their professional performance.

An interesting finding suggested that caseworkers and administrators experienced the highest scores regarding personal emotional impact. Intermediate and low scores were reported by clinicians and jurists respectively. Based on these results, the authors surmised:

> Caseworkers may show the highest potential for burnout because of their prolonged contact with both the victims and the perpetrators of sexual abuse, or because of the personal qualities connected with their initial self-selection for such a challenging and caring profession (p. 202).

INTERVENTION

Recommended interventions for preventing and remediating burnout are generally directed at intrapersonal, interpersonal, and organizational levels (Huebner, 1993). Similar to Violanti (2001), however, Huebner acknowledged the unique experiences of helping professionals and emphasized the need for individual assessments rather than recommending an overarching approach or a one-size-fits-all orientation. In essence, antecedents and manifestations of burnout must be explored at the individual level.

Intrapersonal Intervention

In terms of intrapersonal intervention, strategies involving continuing education, relaxation techniques, time management, realistic goal setting, and recreation have been mentioned (Huebner, 1993; Shapiro, Dorman, Burkey, & Welker, 1999; Thorpe et al., 2001). To sustain a personal and professional self, Skovholt and colleagues (2001) encouraged professionals to (1) maximize success, (2) maintain a development program, (3) increase self-understanding, (4) create a professional greenhouse at work, (5) minimize ambiguous professional loss, and (6) focus on wellness.

Organizational Intervention

The ways that organizations can prevent or alleviate burnout vary and include supervision, support groups and in-service training, staffing and caseload management, and counseling. Each approach is discussed below.

Supervision/Consultation. The importance of effective supervision (Huebner, 1993; Koeske & Kelly, 1995) and consultation (Korkeila et al., 2003) in mitigating professional burnout has been underlined. Huebner (1993) noted that both the professional and the supervisor must remain attentive to burnout and its manifestations. Hawkins (2001) believed supervisors had to be sensitive to issues that contribute to burnout and must be prepared to act to alleviate symptoms.

Support Groups and In-Service Training. Organizational efforts to prevent and combat burnout included the establishment of homogeneous and hetero-geneous support groups. Several authors (Alexander & Hegarty, 2000; Carrilio & Eisenberg, 1984; Evans & Villavisanis, 1997; Huebner, 1993; Korkeila et al., 2003; Shoptaw et al., 2000) remarked that support from others could serve as a mediator of stress reactions and reduce the sense of isolation. Garrett and McDaniel (2001) recommended administrators could promote work environments that reduce workplace uncertainty and increase supervisor support.

In-service courses that are designed to bolster self-esteem and clinical skills have been suggested (Shoptaw et al., 2000; Thorpe et al., 2001). Along a similar vein, Gundersen (2001) identified additional ways to prevent or deal with burnout and included panel and group discussions, conferences, retreats, and self-care strategies. The latter strategy involves appropriate rest, exercise, and personal time. Stress management courses focusing specifically on irrational thinking (Balevre, 2001) or thought management (Potter, 1983) have been recommended. Morgan, Van Haveren, and Pearson (2002) supported the idea of instituting annual training with a focus on sources and symptoms of burnout. These authors also suggested increasing incentives for professionals who con-tinue their education. Finally Evans and Villavisanis (1997) promoted encouragement exchange and wrote, "The purpose of encouragement is to promote and activate the social interest and psychological hardiness of the individual while welcoming him or her into the human community" (p. 342). Encouragement exchange utilizes positive group dynamics and warm-up activities.

Staffing and Caseload Management. Workplace interventions include improved staffing (Aiken et al., 2002), job description modifications, caseload downsizing (Zaslove, 2001), and caseload management (Gundersen, 2001; Hope, 2000). Training in communication and time management skills have also been recommended (Korkeila et al., 2003).

Counseling Services. Hawkins (2001) touted the value of employee assistance programs. In his opinion, such programs provided an important outlet where professionals could seek help.

SUMMARY

Burnout is an established construct that has not progressed in the area of evaluation. In fact, only two inventories and two scales appear in the literature. This is surprising when considering this construct's fanfare and the available information regarding helping professional burnout.

Similar to other forms of helping professional psychological injury, it has been suggested that individual uniqueness be considered when intervening at the intrapersonal, interpersonal, and organizational levels. Readers who are interested in pursuing additional information must rely on books and journal articles.

EVALUATION RESOURCES

Inventories

Burnout Potential Inventory

Potter, B. (1998). *Overcoming job burnout: How to renew enthusiasm for work.* Berkeley, CA: Ronin.

Maslach Burnout Inventory

Maslach, C., Jackson, S., & Schwab, R. (1996). Maslach Burnout Inventory-Educators Survey (MBI-ES). In C. Maslach, S. Jackson, & M. Leiter (Eds.), *MBI Manual* (3rd ed.). Palo Alto, CA: Consulting Psychologists Press.

Oldenburg Burnout Inventory

Demerouti, E., Bakker, A., Vardakou, I., & Kantas, A. (2003). The convergent validity of two burnout instruments: A multitrait-multimethod analysis. *European Journal of Psychological Assessment, 19,* 12–23.

Scales

The Staff Burnout Scale

Jones, J. (1980). *The Staff Burnout Scale for health professionals.* Park Ridge, IL: London House Press.

The Tedium Scale

Pines, A., Aronson, E., Kafry, D. (1981). *Burnout: From tedium to personal growth.* New York: Free Press.

INFORMATION RESOURCES

Books

Cherniss, C. (1995). *Beyond burnout: Helping teachers, nurses, therapists, and lawyers recover from stress and disillusionment*. New York: Routledge.

Freudenberger, H., & Richelson, G. (1980). *Burnout*. New York: Bantam Books.

Gillespie, D. (1987). *Burnout among social workers*. Binghamton, NY: Haworth.

Maslach, C. (1982). *Burnout: The cost of caring*. Upper Saddle River, NJ: Prentice Hall.

Maslach, C., & Leiter, M. (1997). *The truth about burnout: How organizations cause personal stress*. San Francisco, CA: Jossey-Bass.

Moracco, J. (1993). *Therapist burnout: Descriptions and strategies*. Cincinnati, OH: Anderson.

Skovholt, T. (2000). *The resilient practitioner: Burnout prevention for counselors, therapists, teachers, and health professionals*. Boston, MA: Allyn & Bacon.

Van Dongen, E., & Van Dis, H. (Eds.). (1994). *Burnout in HIV/AIDS health care and support: Impact for professionals and volunteers*. Amsterdam: Amsterdam University Press.

Common Psychological Injury Constructs

The following constructs are commonly used in the literature when describing how helping professionals can be affected by their work. By no means should this list be considered exhaustive. Furthermore, additional constructs exist in the literature (e.g., cumulative trauma [Lourie, 1996]) but refer to trauma experienced by victims. As noted in the proceeding list, constructs are often used synonymously.

BURDEN/DISTRESS/STRAIN RELATED

Caregiver Burden — Involves day-to-day adjustment and change and could prevent caregivers from attending to their own needs (Sisk, 2000).

Caregiver Strain — The persistent hardships or the physical, psychological, social, financial, and emotional responses that can be experienced by family members when providing continuing and supportive care (Chen & Hu, 2002).

Emotional Contagion — The sharing or taking-on the emotion of another person (Omdahl & O'Donnell 1999).

Professional Distress — The result of an unresolved personal problem(s) that can potentially lead to impairment (O'Connor, 2001).

STRESS RELATED

Acute stress disorder — "The development of characteristic anxiety, dissociative, and other symptoms that occur within 1 month after exposure to an extreme traumatic stressor" (American Psychiatric Association, 2000, p. 429).

Compassion stress — "… is the residue of emotional energy from the empathic response to the client and is the on-going demand for action to relieve the suffering of a client" (Figley, 2002, p. 1437).

Critical incident stress — Specific, often unexpected, time-limited events that may involve loss or threat to personal goals or well-being, and may represent a potential turning point in the person's life (Everly, Flannery, & Mitchell, 2000, p. 24).

Delayed stress reaction — A chronic form of posttraumatic stress disorder (Kolb, 1983).

Gross stress — "Stress which threatens a vital goal or need, such as per-sonal tragedy, war, or environmental disaster" (Messervy, 1978, p. 28).

Persistent stress reaction — Stress that is described as lingering and chronic (Archibald & Tuddenham, 1965).

Posttraumatic stress disorder — "The development of characteristic symptoms fol-lowing exposure to an extreme traumatic stressor involving direct personal experience of an event that involves actual or threatened death or serious injury, or other threat to one's physical integrity; or witnessing an event that involves death, injury, or a threat to the physical integrity of another person; or learning about unexpected or violent death, serious harm, or threat of death or injury experienced by a family member or other close associate" (American Psychiatric Association, 2000, p. 424).

Primary traumatic stress — "A reaction a person experiences when something bad happens to her or him" (Nelson-Gardell & Harris, 2003, p. 6).

Secondary catastrophic stress reaction — The empathic induction of a family mem-ber's experiences results in considerable emotional upset (Figley, 1995a, p. 4).

Secondary traumatic stress (STS) — A term used synonymously with secondary traumatic stress disorder (O'Halloran, 2001). The natural consequent behaviors and emotions resulting from knowing about a traumatizing event experienced by a significant other — the stress resulting from helping or wanting to help a traumatized or suffering person (Figley, 1995a, p. 7).

Secondary traumatic stress disorder (STSD) — "… is a syndrome of symptoms nearly identical to PTSD, except that exposure to knowledge about a trau-matizing event experienced by a significant other is associated with the set of STSD symptoms, and PTSD symptoms are directly connected to the sufferer, the person experiencing primary traumatic stress" (Figley, 1995a, p. 8).

Stress — "A situation in which the challenges or threats facing the individual exceeds his or her estimated coping mechanisms" (Stoyva & Carlson, 1993, p. 729).

TRAUMA RELATED

Direct trauma — Events directed at a professional that can overwhelm him or her and result in trauma effects (Horwitz, 1998).

Indirect trauma — Events directed at clients that can have a traumatic effect on professionals, "... stemming from either the nature of the event or from emotional contagion" (Horwitz, 1998, p. 367).

Psychotraumatology — "... the study of psychological trauma, more specifically, the study of the processes and factors that lie antecedent to, concomitant with, and subsequent to psychological trauma" (Everly, 1993, p. 270).

Secondary trauma — "A phenomenon which hypothesizes that previously nontraumatized persons acquire characteristic trauma-like responses by having continued contact with those who have endured highly stressful events" (Motta, Joseph, Rose, Suozzi, & Leiderman, 1997, p. 895).

Secondary traumatization — The relationship between a parent's traumatic experiences and subsequent stress disorder and problems exhibited by offspring (Rosenheck & Nathan, 1985).

Systemic traumatization — A term used synonymously with secondary traumatic stress disorder (Figley, 1995b).

Trauma — "... the unique individual experience, associated with an event or enduring conditions, in which (1) the individual's ability to integrate affective experience is overwhelmed or (2) the individual experiences a threat to life or bodily integrity" (Pearlman & Saakvitne, 1995, p.60).

Traumatic neurosis — "... a form of hysteria and the symptoms a consequence of phsyiologic brain dysfunction caused by terror and the memory of the trauma" (Modlin, 1983, p. 662).

Type I trauma — A single unanticipated traumatic event that involves, "... full, detailed memories, 'omens,' and misperceptions" (Terr, 1991, p. 10).

Type II trauma — Long-standing or repeated exposure to extreme external events that involve, "... denial and numbing, self-hypnosis and dissociation, and rage" (Terr, 1991, p. 10).

Vicarious traumatization — "The transformation in the inner experience of the therapist that comes about as a result of the empathic engagement with clients' trauma material" (Pearlman & Saakvitne, 1995, p. 31).

EMPATHY RELATED

Empathic ability — "... is the aptitude of the psychotherapist for noticing the pain of others" (Figley, 2002, p. 1436).

Empathic concern — A concern for the well-being of another that does not require sharing emotion (Omdahl & O'Donnell, 1999).

Empathic engagement — The process of empathizing with traumatized clients (Nelson-Gardell & Harris, 2003).

Empathy fatigue — Transcends burnout and can emerge suddenly with little warn-
ing as an unhealthy form of countertransference (Stebnicki, 2000).

Empathic response — "... the extent to which the psychotherapist makes an effort to
reduce the suffering of the sufferer through empathic understanding. This
insight into feelings, thoughts, and behaviors of the client is achieved by
projecting one's self into the perspective of the client" (Figley, 2002, p. 1437)

Empathic strain — Empathic strain is a rupture in empathy resulting in a loss of an
effective therapeutic role (Jones 2000).

COUNTERTRANSFERENCE

Countertransference — "(1) the affective, ideational, and physical responses a therapist has to her client, his clinical material, transference, and reenactments,
and (2) the therapist's conscious and unconscious defenses against the
affects, intrapsychic conflicts, and associations aroused by the former"
(Pearlman & Saakvitne, 1995, p. 23).

Traumatic countertransference — A process where a client's trauma story revives
personal traumatic experiences that a therapist may have suffered in the past
(Herman, 1992).

BURNOUT

Burnout — "...a state of physical, emotional and mental exhaustion caused by long
term involvement in emotionally demanding situations" (Pines & Aronson,
1988, p. 9).

REFERENCES

American Psychiatric Association (2000). *Diagnostic and statistical manual of mental disorders*
(4th ed.). Washington, DC: Author.

Archibald, H., & Tuddenham, R. (1965). Persistent stress reaction after combat: A 20 year
follow-up. *Archives of General Psychiatry, 12*, 475–481.

Chen, M., & Hu, L. (2002). The generalizability of Caregiver Strain Index in family caregivers of cancer patients. *International Journal of Nursing Studies, 39*, 823–830.

Everly, G. (1993). Psychotraumatology: A two-factor formulation of posttraumatic stress.
Integrative Physiological and Behavioral Science, 28, 270–278.

Everly, G., Flannery, R., & Mitchell, J. (2000). Critical incident stress management (CISM): A
review of the literature. *Aggression and Violent Behavior, 5*, 23–40.

Figley, C. (Ed.). (1995a). *Compassion fatigue: Coping with secondary traumatic stress disorder in
those who treat the traumatized*. New York: Brunner/Mazel.

Figley, C. (1995b). Compassion fatigue as secondary traumatic stress disorder: An overview. In C. Figley (Ed.), *Compassion fatigue: Coping with secondary traumatic stress disorder in those who treat the traumatized* (pp. 1–20). New York: Brunner/Mazel.

Figley, C. (2002). Compassion fatigue: Psychotherapists' chronic lack of self care. *In Session:
Psychotherapy in Practice, 58*, 1433–1441.

Herman, J. (1992). *Trauma and recovery: The aftermath of violence — from domestic abuse to political terror.* New York: Basic Books.

Horwitz, M. (1998). Social worker trauma: Building resilience in child protection social workers. *Smith College Studies in Social Work, 68,* 363–377.

Jones, K. (2000). Counselor reactions to clients traumatized by violence. In D. Sandhu (Ed.), *Faces of violence: Psychological correlates, concepts and intervention strategies* (pp. 379–388). Huntington, NY: Nova Science.

Kolb, L. (1983). Return of the repressed: Delayed stress reaction to war. *Journal of the American Academy of Psychoanalysis, 11,* 531–545.

Lourie, J. (1996). Cumulative trauma: The nonproblem problem. *Transactional Analysis Journal, 26,* 276–283.

Messervy, T. (1978). The recoil phase of the gross stress reaction and its therapy. *Psychiatric Forum, 7,* 28–32.

Modlin, H. (1983). Traumatic neurosis and other injuries. *Psychiatric Clinics of North America, 6,* 661–682.

Motta, R., Joseph, J., Rose, R., Suozzi, J., & Leiderman, L. (1997). Secondary trauma: Assessing intergenerational transmission of war experiences with a Modified Stroop Procedure. *Journal of Clinical Psychology, 53,* 895–903.

Nelson-Gardell, D., & Harris, D. (2003). Child abuse history, secondary traumatic stress, and child welfare workers. *Child Welfare, LXXXII,* 5–26.

O'Connor, M. (2001). On the etiology and effective management of professional distress and impairment among psychologists. *Professional Psychology: Research and Practice, 32,* 345–350.

O'Halloran, S. (2001). Secondary traumatic stress in the classroom: Ameliorating stress in graduate students. *Teaching of Psychology, 28 (2).* Retrieved December 23, 2003, from http://web5.epnet.com.

Omdahl, B., & O'Donnell, C. (1999). Emotional contagion, empathic concern and communicative responsiveness as variables affecting nurses' stress and occupational commitment. *Journal of Advanced Nursing, 29,* 1351–1360.

Pearlman, L., & Saakvitne, K. (1995). *Trauma and the therapist: Countertransference and vicarious traumatization in psychotherapy with incest survivors.* New York: Norton.

Pines, A., & Aronson, E. (1988). *Career burnout: Causes and cures* (2nd ed.). New York: Free Press.

Rosenheck, R., & Nathan, P. (1985). Secondary traumatization in children of Vietnam veterans. *Hospital and Community Psychiatry, 36,* 538–539.

Sisk, R. (2000). Caregiver burden and health promotion. *International Journal of Nursing Studies, 37,* 37–43.

Stebnicki, M. (2000). Stress and grief reactions among rehabilitation professionals: Dealing effectively with empathy fatigue. *Journal of Rehabilitation, 66,* 23–30.

Stoyva, J., & Carlson, J. (1993). A coping/rest model of relaxation and stress management. In L. Goldberger and S. Breznitz (Eds.), *Handbook of stress: Theoretical and clinical aspects* (2nd ed., pp. 724–756). New York: Free Press.

Terr, L. (1991). Childhood trauma: An outline and overview. *American Journal of Psychiatry, 148,* 10–20.

APPENDIX *B*

Journals

The following journals are not directly related to a specific psychological injury construct but may contain information regarding how helping professionals can be affected by their work.

Australian Journal of Disaster and Trauma Studies. URL: http://massey.ac.nz/~trauma.

Journal of Aggression, Maltreatment, and Trauma. URL: http://www.haworthpress.com.

Journal of Threat Assessment. URL: http://www.haworthpressinc.com.

Journal of Trauma and Dissociation. URL: http://www.issd.org/indexpage/jtauthorinfo.html.

Journal of Trauma Practice. URL: http://www.haworthpressinc.com.

Journal of Trauma, Violence, and Abuse. URL: http://www.sage-pub.co.uk.

Journal of Traumatic Stress. URL: http://www.istss.or/Pubs/pubs.html.

Trauma Response. URL: http://www.aaets.or/trresp.htm.

APPENDIX C

Associations

The following organizations are not directly related to a specific psychological injury construct but may address how helping professionals can be affected by their work.

Association of Traumatic Stress Specialists. URL: http://www.atss-hq.com.
Canadian Traumatic Stress Network. URL: http://www.ctsn.rcst.ca.
European Society for Traumatic Stress Studies. URL: http://www.estss.org.
Sidran Traumatic Stress Foundation. URL: http://www.sidran.org.
The American Academy of Experts in Traumatic Stress, Inc. URL: http://www.aaets.org.

References

INTRODUCTION

American Psychiatric Association (2000). *Diagnostic and statistical manual of mental disorders* (4th ed.). Washington, DC: Author.

Anshel, M. (2000). A conceptual model and implications for coping with stressful events in police work. *Criminal Justice & Behavior, 27,* 375–400.

Cardena, E. (2001). Evaluation of post-traumatic stress disorders. *Military Medicine, 166,* 53–54.

Donovan, D. (1991). Traumatology: A field whose time has come. *Journal of Traumatic Stress, 4,* 433–436.

Donovan, D. (1993). Traumatology: What's in a name? *Journal of Traumatic Stress, 6,* 409–411.

Ebsco Publishing (2003). www.epnet.com.

Gist, R., & Woodall, S. (1998). Social science versus social movements: The origins and natural history of debriefing. *Australasian Journal of Disaster and Trauma Studies, 2 (1).* Retrieved June 5, 2003, from http://www.massey.ac.nz/~trauma.

Green, B. (1990). Defining trauma: Terminology and generic stressor dimensions. *Journal of Applied Social Psychology, 20,* 1632–1642.

Harvey, A., & Bryant, R. (2002). Acute stress disorder: A synthesis and critique. *Psychological Bulletin, 128,* 886–902.

Lerner, M., & Shelton, R. (2001). *Acute traumatic stress management (ATSM): Addressing emergent psychological needs during traumatic events.* Commack, NY: American Academy of Experts in Traumatic Stress.

Pontius, E. (1993). Acute traumatic stress: Guidelines for treating mass-causality survivors from the Persian Gulf war. *NCPTSD Clinical Quarterly, 3 (1).* Retrieved May 26, 2003, from http://www.ncptsd.org/publications/cq/v3/n1/pontius.html.

Published International Literature on Traumatic Stress (PILOTS). (2003). http://www.ncptsd.org/research/pilots/index.html.

Robins, L. (1990). Steps toward evaluating post-traumatic stress reaction as a psychiatric disorder. *Journal of Applied Social Psychology, 20,* 1674–1677.

Sabin-Farrell, R., & Turpin, G. (2003). Vicarious traumatization: Implications for the mental health of health workers? *Clinical Psychology Review, 23,* 449–480.

Schnitt, J. (1993). Traumatic stress studies: What's in a name? *Journal of Traumatic Stress, 6,* 405–408.

Sexton, L. (1999). Vicarious traumatisation of counsellors and effects on their workplaces. *British Journal of Guidance and Counselling, 27,* 393–404.

Volpe, J. (1996). Traumatic stress: An overview. *Trauma Response, 3 (2).* Retrieved May 26, 2003, from http://www.aaets.org/arts/art1.htm.

Waters, J. (2002). Moving forward from September 11: A stress/crisis/trauma response model. *Brief Treatments and Crisis Intervention, 2,* 55–74.

CHAPTER 1 TRAUMATOLOGY: AN OVERVIEW

American Psychiatric Association. (1994). *Diagnostic and statistical manual of mental disorders* (4th ed.). Washington, D.C.: Author.

Arvay, M., & Uhlemann, M. (1996). Counsellor stress and impairment in the field of trauma. *Canadian Journal of Counselling, 30,* 193–210.

Babington, A. (1997). *Shell-shock: A history of the changing attitudes of war neurosis.* London: Leo Cooper.

Baird, S., & Jenkins, S. (2003). Vicarious traumatization, secondary traumatic stress, and burnout in sexual assault and domestic violence agency staff. *Violence and Victims, 18,* 71–86.

Ben-Ezra, M. (2002). Trauma 4,000 years ago. *American Journal of Psychiatry, 159,* 1437.

Benatar, M. (2000). A qualitative study of the effect of a history of childhood sexual abuse on therapists who treat survivors of sexual abuse. *Journal of Trauma & Dissociation, 1,* 9–28.

Birmes, P., Hatton, L., Brunet, A., & Schmitt, L. (2003). Early historical literature for post-traumatic symptomatology. *Stress and Health, 19,* 17–26.

Bride, B., Robinson, M., Yegidis, B., & Figley, C. (2003). Development and validation of the secondary traumatic stress scale. *Research on Social Work Practice, 13,* 1–16.

Briere, J. (1992). *Child abuse trauma: Theory and treatment of the lasting effects.* Newbury Park, CA: Sage.

Cain, N. (2000). Psychotherapists with personal histories of psychiatric hospitalization: Countertransference in wounded healers. *Psychiatric Rehabilitation Journal, 24,* 22–29.

Carson, M., Paulus, L., Lasko, N., Metzger, L., Wolfe, J., Orr, S., & Pitman, R. (2000). Psycho-physiologic assessment of posttraumatic stress disorder in Vietnam nurse veterans who witnessed injury or death. *Journal of Consulting or Clinical Psychology, 68,* 890–897.

Chen, M., & Hu, L. (2002). The generalizability of Caregiver Strain Index in family caregivers of cancer patients. *International Journal of Nursing Studies, 39,* 823–830.

Collins, S., & Long, A. (2003). Too tired to care? The psychological effects of working with trauma. *Journal of Psychiatric and Mental Health Nursing, 10,* 17–27.

Cornille, T., & Woodward Meyers, T. (1999). Secondary traumatic stress among child protective service workers: Prevalence, severity, and predictive factors. *Traumatology 5* (4). Retrieved May 19, 2003, from http://www.fsu.edu/~trauma/v6ia3.htm.

Culpin, M. (1920). Psychology of Effort Syndrome. *The Lancet, 2,* 184–186.

DeFazio, V. (1978). Dynamic perspectives on the nature and effects of combat stress. In C. Figley (Ed.), *Stress disorders among Vietnam veterans: Theory, research, and treatment* (pp. 23–42). New York: Brunner/Mazel.

Dunning, C., & Silva, M. (1980). Disaster-induced trauma in rescue workers. *Victimology: An International Journal, 5,* 287–297.

Eidelson, R., D'Alessio, G., & Eidelson, J. (2003). The impact of September 11 on psychologists. *Professional Psychology: Research and Practice, 34,* 144–150.

Elliott, D., & Guy, J. (1993). Mental health professionals versus non-mental health professionals: Childhood trauma and adult functioning. *Professional Psychology: Research and Practice, 24,* 83–90.

Everstine, D., & Everstine, L. (1993). *The trauma response: Treatment for emotional injury.* New York: Norton.

Feinberg, T. (2002). Caring for caregivers after 9/11. *Education Digest, 67,* 8–11.

Figley, C. (Ed.). (1978). *Stress disorders among Vietnam veterans: Theory, research and treatment.* New York: Brunner/Mazel.

Figley, C. (1989a). *Helping traumatized families.* San Francisco: Jossey-Bass.

Figley, C. (1989b). *Treating stress in families.* New York: Brunner/Mazel.

Figley, C. (1995a). Systemic traumatization: Secondary traumatic stress disorder in family therapists. In R. Mikesell, D. Lusterman, & S. McDaniel (Eds.), *Integrating family therapy: Handbook of family psychology and systems theory* (pp. 571–581). Washington, DC: American Psychological Association.

Figley, C. (Ed.). (1995b). *Compassion fatigue: Coping with secondary traumatic stress disorder in those who treat the traumatized.* New York: Brunner/Mazel.

Figley, C. (Ed.). (1998). *Burnout in families: The systemic costs of caring*. New York: CRC Press.

Follette, V., Poluusny, M., & Milbeck, K. (1994). Mental health and law enforcement professionals: Trauma history, psychological symptoms, and impact of providing services to child sexual abuse perpetrators. *Professional Psychology: Research and Practice, 25,* 275–282.

Gal, R. (1998). Colleagues in distress: 'Helping the helpers'. *International Review of Psychiatry, 10,* 234–238.

Ghahramanlou, M., & Brodbeck, C. (2000). Predictors of secondary trauma in sexual assault trauma counselors. *International Journal of Emergency Mental Health, 2,* 229–240.

Green, B. (1990). Defining trauma: Terminology and generic stressor dimensions. *Journal of Applied Social Psychology, 20,* 1632–1642.

Haley, S. (1974). When the patient reports atrocities: Specific treatment considerations of the Vietnam veteran. *Archives of General Psychiatry, 30,* 191–196.

Harbert, K., & Hunsinger, M. (1991). The impact of traumatic stress reactions on caregivers. *Journal of the American Academy of Physician Assistants, 4,* 384–394.

Herman, J. (1992). *Trauma and recovery: The aftermath of violence — from domestic abuse to political terror*. New York: Basic Books.

Horwitz, M. (1998). Social worker trauma: Building resilience in child protection social workers. *Smith College Studies in Social Work, 68,* 363–377.

Howell, J. (1985). Soldier's heart: The redefinition of heart disease and specialty formation in early twentieth century Great Britain. *Medical History, Supplement No. 5,* 34–52.

Hyams, K., Wignall, S., & Roswell, R. (1996). War syndromes and their evaluation: From the U.S. Civil War to the Persian Gulf War. *Annals of Internal Medicine, 125,* 398–405.

Janik, J. (1995). Overwhelmed corrections workers can seek therapy. *Corrections Today, 57 (7).* Retrieved December 27, 2003, from http://web24.epnet.com/citation.

Jenkins, S., & Baird, S. (2002). Secondary traumatic stress and vicarious trauma: A validation study. *Journal of Traumatic Stress, 15,* 423–432.

Joinson, C. (1992). Coping with compassion fatigue. *Nursing, 22,* 116–121.

Kassam-Adams, N. (1995). The risks of treating sexual trauma: Stress and secondary stress among therapists. In B. Stamm (Ed.), *Secondary traumatic stress: Self-care issues for clinicians, researchers, and educators* (pp. 37–50). Lutherville, MD: Sidran Press.

Klingman, A. (2002). From supportive-listening to a solution-focused intervention for counsellors dealing with political trauma. *British Journal of Guidance & Counselling, 30,* 247–259.

Kormos, H. (1978). The nature of combat stress. In C. Figley (Ed.), *Stress disorders among Vietnam veterans: Theory, research and practice* (pp. 3–22). New York: Brunner/Mazel.

Larson, D. (1987). Internal stressors of nursing: Helper secrets. *Journal of Psychosocial Nursing, 25,* 20–27.

Lewis, T. (1941). *The soldier's heart and effort syndrome*. London: Shaw and Sons.

McCann, I., & Pearlman, L. (1990). Vicarious traumatization: A framework for understanding the psychological effects of working with victims. *Journal of Traumatic Stress, 3,* 131–149.

Miller, G., Britton, T., Wagner, A., & Gridley, B. (1998). A framework for understanding the wounded healers. *Counseling and Values, 42,* 124–133.

Milstein, J., Gerstenberger, E., & Barton, S. (2002). Healing the caregiver. *Journal of Alternative and Complementary Medicine, 8,* 917–920.

Morrissette, P. (2001). *Self-supervision: A primer for counselors and helping professionals*. Philadelphia, PA: Brunner-Routledge.

Morrissette, P., & Naden, M. (1998). An interactional view of traumatic stress among First Nations counselors. *Journal of Family Psychotherapy, 9,* 43–60.

Motta, R., Kefer, J., Hertz, M., & Hafeez, S. (1999). Initial evaluation of the secondary trauma questionnaire. *Psychological Reports, 85,* 997–1002.

Nelson-Gardell, D., & Harris, D. (2003). Child abuse history, secondary traumatic stress, and child welfare workers. *Child Welfare, LXXXII,* 5–26.

Nelson, B., & Schwerdtfeger, K. (2002). Trauma to one family member affects entire family. *Traumatic Stress Points, 16 (7).* Retrieved December 27, 2003, from http://www.cja.org/aboutCJA/CJA_News/CJA_Press_Stress_Spr02.htm.

O'Connor, M. (2001). On the etiology and effective management of professional distress and impairment among psychologists. *Professional Psychology: Research and Practice, 32,* 345–350.

Ortlepp, K., & Friedman, M. (2002). Prevalence and correlates of secondary traumatic stress in workplace lay trauma counselors. *Journal of Traumatic Stress, 15,* 213–222.

Parson, E. (1985). Ethnicity and traumatic stress: The intersecting point in psychotherapy. In C. Figley (Ed.), *Trauma and its wake: The study and treatment of post-traumatic stress disorder.* New York: Brunner/Mazel.

Pearlman, L., & MacIan, P. (1995). Vicarious traumatization: An empirical study of the effects of trauma work on trauma therapists. *Professional Psychology: Research and Practice, 26,* 558–565.

Pearlman, L., & Saakvitne, K. (1995). *Trauma and the therapist: Countertransference and vicarious traumatization in psychotherapy with incest survivors.* New York: Norton.

Peeples, K. (2000). Interview with Charles R. Figley: Burnout in families and implications for the profession. *The Family Journal, 8,* 203–206.

Pfifferling, J., & Gilley, K. (2000). Overcoming compassion fatigue. *Family Practice Management, 7, (4).* Retrieved December 27, 2003, from http://web24.epnet.com/citation.

Pope, K., & Feldman-Summers, S. (1992). National survey of psychologists' sexual and physical abuse history and their evaluation of training and competence in these areas. *Professional Psychology: Research and Practice, 23,* 353–361.

Raingruber, B., & Kent, M. (2003). Attending to embodied responses: A way to identify practice-based and human meanings associated with secondary trauma. *Qualitative Health Research, 13,* 449–468.

Raphael, B., Singh, B., Bradbury, L., & Lambert, F. (1983). Who helps the helpers? The effects of a disaster on the rescue workers. *OMEGA, 14,* 9–20.

Regehr, C., Goldberg, G., Glancy, G., & Knott, T. (2002). Posttraumatic symptoms and disability in paramedics. *Canadian Journal of Psychiatry, 47,* 953–959.

Remer, R., & Ferguson, R. (1995). Becoming a secondary survivor of sexual assault. *Journal of Counseling and Development, 73,* 407–413.

Remer, R., & Ferguson, R. (1998). Treating traumatized partners: Producing secondary survivors of PTSD. In C. Figley (Ed.), *Burnout in families: The systemic costs of caring* (pp. 139–170). New York: CRC Press.

Saakvitne, K. (2002). Shared trauma: The therapist's increased vulnerability. *Psychoanalytic Dialogues, 12,* 443–449.

Schauben, L., & Frazier, P. (1995). Vicarious trauma: The effects on female counselors working with sexual violence survivors. *Psychology of Women Quarterly, 19,* 49–54.

Schnitt, J. (1993). Traumatic stress studies: What's in a name? *Journal of Traumatic Stress, 6,* 405–408.

Scott, M., & Stradling, S. (1994). *Counseling for post-traumatic stress disorder.* London: Sage.

Shakespeare-Finch, J., Smith, S., & Obst, P. (2002). Trauma, coping resources, and family functioning in emergency services personnel: A comparative study. *Work & Stress, 16,* 275–282.

Shepherd, M., & Hodgkinson, P. (1990). The hidden victims of disaster: Helper stress. *Stress Medicine, 6,* 29–35.

Sisk, R. (2000). Caregiver burden and health promotion. *International Journal of Nursing Studies, 37,* 37–43.

Stamm. B. (1997). Work-related secondary traumatic stress. *NCPTSD Research Quarterly, 8,* 1–6.

Steed, L., & Bicknell, J. (2001). Trauma and the therapist: The experience of therapists work-ing with the perpetrators of sexual abuse. *Australasian Journal of Disaster and Trauma Studies, 1 (3)*. Retrieved June 5, 2003, from http://www.massey.ac.nz/~trauma.

Waters, J. (2002). Moving forward from September 11: A stress/crisis/trauma response model. *Brief Treatments and Crisis Intervention, 2,* 55–74.

Waysman, M., Mikulincer, M., Solomon, Z., & Weisenberg, M. (1993). Secondary traumati-zation among wives of posttraumatic combat veterans: A family typology. *Journal of Family Psychology, 7,* 104–118.

Wee, D., & Myers, D. (2003). Compassion satisfaction, compassion fatigue, and critical inci-dent stress management. *International Journal of Emergency Mental Health, 5,* 33–37.

Weisaeth, L. (2002). The European history of psychotraumatology. *Journal of Traumatic Stress, 15,* 443–452.

Williams, M., & Sommer, J. (Eds.). (1994). *Handbook of post-traumatic stress therapy.* Westport, CT: Greenwood.

Wilson, J. (1994a). The historical evolution of PTSD diagnostic criteria: From Freud to DSM-IV. *Journal of Traumatic Stress, 7,* 681–698.

Wilson, J. (1994b). The need for an integrative theory of post-traumatic stress disorder. In M. Williams and J. Sommer (Eds.). *Handbook of posttraumatic stress therapy* (pp. 3–18). Westport, CT: Greenwood Press.

Yassen, J. (1993). Groupwork with clinicians who have a history of trauma. *NCPTSD Clini-cal Newsletter, 3, (2)*. Retrieved May 26, 2003, from http://ncpts.org/publications/cq/v3/n2yassen.hmtl.

Yassen, J. (1995). Preventing secondary traumatic stress disorder. In C. Figley (Ed.), *Compas-sion fatigue: Coping with secondary traumatic stress disorder in those who treat the trauma-tized* (pp. 179–208). New York: Brunner/Mazel.

CHAPTER 2 STRESS

Abdollahi, M. (2002). Understanding police stress research. *Journal of Forensic Psychology Practice, 2,* 1–24.

Anshel, M. (2000). A conceptual model and implications for coping with stressful events in police work. *Criminal Justice & Behavior, 27,* 375–400.

Baker, S., & Williams, K. (2001). Short communication: Relation between social problem-solving appraisals, work stress and psychological distress in male firefighters. *Stress and Health, 17,* 219–229.

Bennett, P., Lowe, R., Matthews, V., Dourali, M. & Tattersall, A. (2001). Stress in nurses: Coping, managerial support and work demand. *Stress and Health, 17,* 55–63.

Breznitz, S., & Goldberger, L. (1993). Stress research at a crossroads. In L. Goldberger and S. Breznitz (Eds.), *Handbook of stress: Theoretical and clinical aspects* (pp. 3–6). New York: Free Press.

Buchanan, G., Stephens, C., & Long, N. (2001). Traumatic experiences of new recruits and serving police. *Australasian Journal of Disaster and Trauma Studies, 2 (1)*. Retrieved May 26, 2003, from http://www.massey.ac.nz/~trauma.

Callaghan, P., Tak-Ying, S., & Wyatt, P. (2000). Factors related to stress and coping among Chinese nurses in Hong Kong. *Journal of Advanced Nursing, 31,* 1518–1527.

Childress, R., Talucci, V., Wood, J. (1999). Fighting the enemy within: Helping officers deal with stress. *Corrections Today, 61,* 70–73.

Coffey, M. (1999). Stress and burnout in forensic community mental health nurses: An investigation of its causes and effects. *Journal of Psychiatric and Mental Health Nursing, 6,* 433–443.

Coffey, M., & Coleman, M. (2001). The relationship between support and stress in forensic community mental health nursing. *Journal of Advanced Nursing, 34*, 397–408.

Curran, S. (2003). Separating fact from fiction about police stress. *Behavioral Health Management, 23*, 38–40.

Edwards, D., Burnard, P., Coyle, D., Fothergill, A., & Hannigan, B. (2000). Stressors, moderators and stress outcomes: Findings from the all-Wales community Mental Health Nurse study. *Journal of Psychiatric and Mental Health Nursing, 7*, 529–537.

Edwards, D., Hannigan, B., Fothergill, A., & Burnard, P. (2002). Stress management for mental health professionals: A review of effective techniques. *Stress and Health, 18*, 203–215.

Edwards, D., & Burnard, P. (2003). A systematic review of stress and stress management interventions for mental health nurses. *Journal of Advanced Nursing, 42*, 169–200.

Escot, C., Artero, S., Gandubert, C., Boulenger, J., & Ritchie, K. (2001). Stress levels in nursing staff working in oncology. *Stress & Health: Journal of the International Society for the Investigation of Stress, 17*, 273–279.

Evans, L. (2002). An exploration of district nurses' perception of occupational stress. *British Journal of Nursing, 11*, 576–585.

Finn, P. (1998). Correctional officer stress: A cause for concern and additional help. *Federal Probation, 62*, 65–75.

Flanagan, N., & Flanagan, T. (2002). An analysis of the relationship between job satisfaction and job stress in correction nurses. *Research in Nursing & Health, 2002, 25*, 282–294.

Gershon, R., Lin, S., & Li, X. (2002). Work stress in aging police officers. *Journal of Occupational Environmental Medicine, 44*, 160–167.

Goldenberg, L., & Breznitz, S. (Eds.). (1993). *Handbook of stress: Theoretical and clinical aspects* (2nd ed.). New York: Free Press.

Happell, B., Pinikahana, J., & Martin, T. (2003). Stress and burnout in forensic psychiatric nursing. *Stress and Health, 19*, 63–68.

Healy C., & McKay, M. (1999). Identifying sources of stress and job satisfaction in the nursing environment. *Australian Journal of Advanced Nursing 17*, 30–35.

Healy, C., & McKay, M. (2000). Nursing stress: The effects of coping strategies and job satisfaction in a sample of Australian nurses. *Journal of Advanced Nursing, 31*, 681–688.

Innes, J., & Slack, J. (1990). Some considerations on personal reactions to emergency stress in employed and volunteer disaster organizational personnel. *International Journal of Mass Emergencies and Disasters, 8*, 379–400.

Kiemle, G. (1994). What's so special about HIV and AIDS? Stresses and strains for clients and counsellors. *British Journal of Guidance and Counselling, 22*, 343–352.

Kipping, C. (2000). Stress in mental health nursing. *International Journal of Nursing Studies, 37*, 207–218.

Kirkcaldy, B., & Siefen, G. (2002). The occupational stress and health outcome profiles of clinical directors in child and adolescent psychiatry. *Stress and Health, 18*, 161–172.

Kluger, M., Townend, K., & Laidlaw, T. (2003). Job satisfaction, stress and burnout in Australian specialist anaesthetists. *Anaesthesia, 58*, 339–345.

Lamberg, L. (1999). "If I work hard(er), I will be loved." Roots of Physician Stress Explored. *Journal of the American Medical Association, 282*, 13–15.

Leary, J., Gallagher, T., Carson, J., Fagin, L., Bartlett, H., & Brown, D. (1995). Stress and coping strategies in community psychiatric nurses: A Q-methodological study. *Journal of Advanced Nursing, 21*, 230–237.

Lert, F., Chastang, J., & Castano, I. (2001). Psychological stress among hospital doctors caring for HIV patients in the late nineties. *Aids Care, 13*, 763–778.

Le Scanff, C., & Taugis, J. (2002). Stress management for police officers. *Journal of Applied Sport Psychology, 14*, 330–343.

Linzer, M., Gerrity, M., Douglas, J., McMurray, J., Williams, E., & Konard, T. (2002). Physician stress: Results from the physician worklife study. *Stress & Health: Journal of the International Society for the Investigation of Stress, 18,* 37–42.

Lloyd, C., King, R., & Chenoweth, L. (2002). Social work, stress and burnout: A review. *Journal of Mental Health, 11,* 255–266.

McGowan B. (2001). Self-reported stress and its effects on nurses. *Nursing Standard, 15,* 33–38.

Moran, C., & Britton, N. (1994). Emergency work experience and reactions to traumatic incidents. *Journal of Traumatic Stress, 7,* 575–585.

O'Halloran, T., & Linton, J. (2000). Stress on the job: Self-care resources for counselors. *Journal of Mental Health Counseling, 22,* 354–364.

Pancheri, P., Martini, A., Tarsitani, L., Rosati, M., Biodi, M., & Tomei, F. (2002). Assessment of subjective stress in the municipal police force of the city of Rome. *Stress and Health, 18,* 127–132.

Patterson, G. (2001). Reconceptualizing traumatic incidents experienced by law enforcement personnel. *Australasian Journal of Disaster and Trauma Studies, 2 (4).* Retrieved June 5, 2003, from http://www.massey.ac.nz/~trauma.

Patterson, G. (2002). Development of a law enforcement stress and coping questionnaire. *Psychological Reports, 90,* 789–799.

Pines, A. (1993). Burnout. In L. Goldberger and S. Breznitz (Eds.), *Handbook of stress: Theoretical and clinical aspects* (2nd ed., pp. 386–402). New York: Free Press.

Pongruengphant, R., & Tyson, P. (2000). When nurses cry: Coping with occupational stress in Thailand. *International Journal of Nursing, 37,* 535–544.

Rodney, V. (2000). Nurse stress associated with aggression in people with dementia: Is relationship to hardiness, cognitive appraisal and coping. *Journal of Advanced Nursing, 31,* 172–180.

Rutter, H., Herzberg, J., & Paice, E. (2002). Stress in doctors and dentists who teach. *Medical Education, 26,* 543–549.

Schmitz, N., Nuemann, W., & Oppermann, R. (2000). Stress, burnout and locus of control in German Nurses. *International Journal of Nursing Studies, 37,* 95–99.

Sharkey, S., & Sharples, A. (2003). The impact on work-related stress of mental health teams following team-based learning on clinical risk management. *Journal of Psychiatric and Mental Health Nursing, 10,* 73–81.

Shipley, P., & Baranski, J. (2002). Police officer performance under stress: A pilot study on the effects of visuo-motor behavior rehearsal. *International Journal of Stress Management, 9,* 71–80.

Slate, R., Johnson, W., & Wells, T. (2000). Probation officer stress: Is there an organizational solution? *Federal Probation, 64,* 56–59.

Sowa, C., & May, K. (1994). Occupational stress within the counseling profession: Implications for counselor training. *Counselor Education and Supervision, 34,* 19–31.

Stoyva, J., & Carlson, J. (1993). A coping/rest model of relaxation and stress management. In L. Goldberger and S. Breznitz (Eds.), *Handbook of stress: Theoretical and clinical aspects* (2nd ed., pp. 724–756). New York: Free Press.

Thompson, B., Kirk–Brown, A., & Brown, D. (2001). Women police: The impact of work stress on family members. In P. Hancock and P. Desmond (Eds.), *Stress, workload, and fatigue* (pp. 200–210). Lawrence, NJ: Erlbaum Associates.

Tyson, P., Pongruengphant, R., & Aggarwal, B. (2002). Coping with organizational stress among hospital nurses in Southern Ontario. *International Journal of Nursing Studies, 39,* 453–459.

Visser, M., Smets, E., Oort, F., & de Haes, H. (2003). Stress, satisfaction and burnout among Dutch medical specialists. *Canadian Medical Association Journal, 168,* 271–275.

Wilson, S., Tinker, R., Becker, L., & Logan, C. (2001). Stress management with law enforcement personnel: A controlled outcome study of EMDR versus a traditional stress management program. *International Journal of Stress Management, 8,* 179–200.

Zhao, J., He, N., & Lovrich, N. (2002). Predicting five dimensions of police officer stress: Looking more deeply into organizational settings for sources of police stress. *Police Quarterly, 5,* 43–63.

CHAPTER 3 ACUTE STRESS DISORDER

American Psychiatric Association (2000). *Diagnostic and statistical manual of mental disorders* (4th ed.). Washington, DC: Author.

Bryant, R., & Harvey, A. (1997). Acute stress disorder: A critical review of diagnostic issues. *Clinical Psychology Review, 17,* 757–773.

Bryant, R., & Harvey, A. (2000). *Acute stress disorder: A handbook of theory, assessment, and treatment.* Washington, DC: American Psychological Association.

Bryant, R. (2000). Acute stress disorder. *PTSD Research Quarterly, 11,* 1–4.

Bryant, R., & Moulds, M. (2000). Acute stress disorder scale: A self-report measure of acute stress disorder. *Psychological Assessment, 12,* 61–69.

Bryant, R., Moulds, M., & Guthrie, R. (2000). Acute stress disorder scale: A self-report measure of acute stress disorder. *Psychological Assessment, 12,* 61–68.

Harvey, A., & Bryant, R. (2002). Acute stress disorder: A synthesis and critique. *Psychological Bulletin, 128,* 886–902.

Koopman, C. (2000). New DSM-IV diagnosis of acute stress disorder. *American Journal of Psychiatry, 157,* 1888.

Shipley, P., & Baranski, J. (2002). Police officer performance under stress: A pilot study on the effects of visuo-motor behavior rehearsal. *International Journal of Stress Management, 9,* 71– 80.

Yeh, C., Leckman, J., Wan, F., Shiah, I., & Lu, R. (2002). Characteristics of acute stress symptoms and nitric oxide concentration in young rescue workers in Taiwan. *Psychiatry Research, 112,* 59–68.

CHAPTER 4 POSTTRAUMATIC STRESS DISORDER

American Psychiatric Association (2000). *Diagnostic and statistical manual of mental disorders* (4th ed.). Washington, DC: Author.

Daly, R. (1983). Samuel Pepys and post-traumatic stress disorder. *British Journal of Psychiatry, 143,* 64–68.

Durham, T., McCammon, S., & Allison, E. (1985). The psychological impact of disaster on rescue personnel. *Annals of Emergency Medicine, 14,* 664–668.

Flannery, R. (1999). Psychological trauma and posttraumatic stress disorder: A review. *International Journal of Emergency Mental Health, 2,* 135–140.

Kitchiner, N., & Aylard, P. (2002). Psychological treatment of post-traumatic stress disorder: A single case study of a UK police office. *Mental Health Practice, 5,* 34–39.

Kohn, C., Hasty, S., & Henderson, C. (2002). Police officers who panic during traumatic event have greatest risk of PTSD. *Pain & Central Nervous System Week,* March 4, 2002. Retrieved June 5, 2003 from http://weblinks1.epnet.com.

Laposa, J., & Alden, L. (2003). Posttraumatic stress disorder in the emergency room: Exploration of a cognitive model. *Behaviour Research and Therapy, 41,* 49–65.

Laposa, J., Alden, L., & Fullerton, L. (2003). Work stress and posttraumatic stress disorder in ED nurses/personnel. *Journal of Emergency Nursing, 29,* 23–28.

Lazarus, R., & Folkman, S. (1984). *Stress, appraisal, and coping*. New York: Springer.

Marshall, R., & Pierce, D. (2000). Implications of recent findings in posttraumatic stress disorder and the role of pharmacotherapy. *Harvard Review of Psychiatry, 7,* 247–256.

McCammon, S., Durham, T., Allison, E., & Williamson, J. (1988). Emergency workers' cognitive appraisal and coping with traumatic events. *Journal of Traumatic Stress, 1,* 353–372.

McFarlane, A., & Bookless, C. (2001). The effect of PTSD on interpersonal relationships: Issues for emergency service workers. *Sexual and Relationship Therapy, 16,* 261–267.

North, C., Tivis, L., McMillen, J., Pfefferbaum, B., Cox, J., Spitznagel, E., Bunch, K., Schorr, J., & Smith, E. (2002a). Coping, functioning, and adjustment of rescue workers after the Oklahoma City bombing. *Journal of Traumatic Stress, 15,* 171–175.

North, C., Tivis, L., McMillen, J., Pfefferbaum, B., Spitznagel, E., Cox, J., Nixon, S., Bunch, K., & Smith, E. (2002b). Psychiatric disorders in rescue workers after the Oklahoma City bombing. *American Journal of Psychiatry, 159,* 857–859.

Renck, B., Weisaeth, L., & Skarbo, S. (2002). Stress reactions in police officers after a disaster rescue operation. *Nordic Journal of Psychiatry, 56,* 7–14.

Saakvitne, K., Tennen, H., & Affleck, G. (1998). Exploring thriving in the context of clinical trauma theory: Constructivist self development theory. *Journal of Social Issues, 54,* 279–299.

Violanti, J. (2001). Posttraumatic stress disorder intervention in law enforcement: Differing perspectives. *The Australasian Journal of Disaster and Trauma Studies, 2 (6).* Retrieved June 5, 2003, from http://www.massey.ac.nz/~trauma.

Wagner, D., Heinrichs, M., & Ehlert, U. (1998). Prevalence of symptoms of posttraumatic stress disorder in German professional firefighters. *American Journal of Psychiatry, 155,* 1727–1732.

CHAPTER 5 COMPASSION FATIGUE/SECONDARY TRAUMATIC STRESS DISORDER

Alpert, J., & Paulson, A. (1990). Graduate-level education and training in child sexual abuse. *Professional Psychology: Research and Practice, 21,* 366–371.

Arvay, M. (2001). Secondary traumatic stress among trauma counsellors: What does the research say? *International Journal for the Advancement of Counselling, 23,* 283–293.

Badger, J. (2001). Understanding secondary traumatic stress. *American Journal of Nursing, 101,* 26–32.

Birck, A. (2002). Secondary traumatization and burnout in professionals working with torture victims. *Traumatology, 7,* 85–90.

Carbonell, J., & Figley, C. (1996). When trauma hits home: Personal trauma and the family therapist. *Journal of Marriage and Family Therapy, 22,* 53–58.

Cloitre, M. (1998). Women and trauma: A clinical forum. *NCPTSD Clinical Quarterly, 8,* 12–13.

Cornille, T., & Woodward Meyers, T. (1999). Secondary traumatic stress among child protective service workers: Prevalence, severity, and predictive factors. *Traumatology 5, (4).* Retrieved May 19, 2003, from http://www.fsu.edu/~trauma/v6ia3.htm.

Dane, B. (2000). Child welfare workers: An innovative approach for interacting with secondary trauma. *Journal of Social Work Education, 36,* 27–38.

Dutlon, M. & Robinstein, F. (1995) Working with people with PTSD: Research implications. In C. Figley (Ed.), *Compassion fatigue: Coping with secondary traumatic disorder in those who treat traumatized* (pp. 82–100). New York: Brunner/Mazel.

Figley, C. (1995a). Systemic traumatization: Secondary traumatic stress disorder in family therapists. In R. Mikesell, D. Lusterman, & S. McDaniel (Eds.), *Integrating family therapy: Handbook of Family Psychology and systems theory* (pp. 571–581). Washington, DC: American Psychological Association.

Figley, C. (Ed.). (1995b). *Compassion fatigue: Coping with secondary traumatic stress disorder in those who treat the traumatized.* New York: Brunner/Mazel.

Figley, C. (2002). Compassion fatigue: Psychotherapist's chronic lack of self-care. *In session: Psychotherapy in Practice, 58,* 1433–1441.

Ghahramanlou, M., & Brodbeck, C. (2000). Predictors of secondary trauma in sexual assault trauma counselors. *International Journal of Emergency Mental Health, 2,* 229–240.

Hesse, A. (2002). Secondary trauma: How working with trauma survivors affects therapists. *Clinical Social Work Journal, 30,* 293–309.

Huggard, P. (2003). Compassion fatigue: How much can I give? *Medical Education, 37,* 163–164.

Inbar, J., & Ganor, M. (2003). Trauma and compassion fatigue: Helping the helpers. *Journal of Jewish Communal Service, 79,* 109–111.

Janik, J. (1995). Overwhelmed corrections workers can seek therapy. *Corrections Today, 57,* 7.

Janoff-Bulman, R. (1985). The aftermath of victimization: Rebuilding shattered assumptions. In C Figley (ed.). *Trauma and its wake: The study of treatment of post-traumatic disorder* (Vol. 1, pp. 15–25). New York: Brunner/Maze.

Joinson, C. (1992). Coping with compassion fatigue. *Nursing, 22,* 116–121.

Jones, K. (2000). Counselor reactions to clients traumatized by violence. In D. Sandhu (Ed.), *Faces of violence: Psychological correlates, concepts and intervention strategies* (pp. 379–388). Huntington, NY: Nova Science.

Kees, N., & Lashwood, P. (1996). Compassion fatigue and school personnel: Remaining open to the affective needs of students. *Educational Horizons, 75,* 41–44.

Leon, A., Altholz, J., & Dziegielewski, S. (1999). Compassion fatigue: Considerations for working with the elderly. *Journal of Geronotological Social Work, 32,* 43–62.

MacLeod, C. (1991). Half a century of research on the Stroop effect: An integrative review. *Psychological Bulletin, 109,* 163–203.

McCammon, S. (1995). Pain pedagogy: Teaching about trauma in academic and training settings. In B. H. Stamm (Ed.), *Secondary traumatic stress: Self-care issues for clinicians, researchers, and educators* (pp. 105–120). Lutherville, MD: Sidran Press.

Milstein, J., Gerstenberger, E., & Barton, S. (2002). Healing the caregiver. *Journal of Alternative and Complementary Medicine, 8,* 917–920.

Motta, R., Joseph, J., Rose, R., Suozzi, J., & Leiderman, L. (1997). Secondary trauma: Assessing intergenerational transmission of war experiences with a Modified Stroop Procedure. *Journal of Clinical Psychology, 53,* 895–903.

Motta, R., Kefer, J., Hertz, M., & Hafeez, S. (1999). Initial evaluation of the secondary trauma questionnaire. *Psychological Reports, 85,* 997–1002.

Nelson-Gardell, D., & Harris, D. (2003). Child abuse history, secondary traumatic stress, and child welfare workers. *Child Welfare, LXXXII,* 5–26.

O'Halloran, S. (2001). Secondary traumatic stress in the classroom: Ameliorating stress in graduate students. *Teaching of Psychology, 28, (2).* Retrieved December 23, 2003, from http://web5.epnet.com

Ortlepp, K., & Friedman, M. (2002). Prevalence and correlates of secondary traumatic stress in workplace lay trauma counselors. *Journal of Traumatic Stress, 15,* 213–222.

Pfifferling, J., & Gilley, K. (2000). Overcoming compassion fatigue. *Family Practice Management, 7,* 39–45.

Pope, K., & Feldman-Summers, S. (1992). National survey of psychologists' sexual and physical abuse history and their evaluation of training and competence in these areas. *Professional Psychology: Research and Practice, 23,* 353–361.

Raingruber, B., & Kent, M. (2003). Attending to embodied responses: A way to identify practice-based and human meanings associated with secondary trauma. *Qualitative Health Research, 13,* 449–468.

Salston, M., & Figley, C. (2003). Secondary traumatic stress effects of working with survivors of criminal victimization. *Journal of Traumatic Stress, 16,* 167–174.

Selye, H. (1974*). Stress without distress.* Philadelphia: Lippincott.

Stebnicki, M. (2000). Stress and grief reactions among rehabilitation professionals: Dealing effectively with empathy fatigue. *Journal of Rehabilitation, 66,* 23–30.

Steed, L., & Bicknell, J. (2001). Trauma and the therapist: The experience of therapists working with the perpetrators of sexual abuse. *Australasian Journal of Disaster and Trauma Studies, 1 (3).* Retrieved June 5, 2003, from http://www.massey.ac.nz/~trauma.

CHAPTER 6 CRITICAL INCIDENT STRESS

Antai-Otong, D. (2001). Critical incident stress debriefing: A health promotion model for workplace violence. *Perspectives in Psychiatric Care, 37,* 125–139.

Bisson, J., Jenkins, P., Alexander, J., & Bannister, C. (1997). Randomized controlled trial of psychological debriefing for victims of acute burn trauma. *British Journal of Psychiatry, 171,* 78–81.

Crawford, K., & Flannery, R. (2002). Critical incident stress management and the Office of the Chief Medical Examiner: Preliminary inquiry. *International Journal of Emergency Mental Health, 4,* 93–97.

Deahl, M. (2000). Psychological debriefing: Controversy and challenge. *Australian and New Zealand Journal of Psychiatry, 34,* 929–939.

Everly, G., Boyle, S., & Lating, J. (1999). The effectiveness of psychological debriefing with vicarious trauma: A meta-analysis. *Stress Medicine, 15,* 229–233.

Everly, G., Flannery, R., & Mitchell, J. (2000). Critical incident stress management (CISM): A review of the literature. *Aggression and Violent Behavior, 5,* 23–40.

Flannery, R. (1999). Psychological trauma and posttraumatic stress disorder: A review. *International Journal of Emergency Mental Health, 2,* 135–140.

Galliano, S. (2002). Debriefing reconsidered. *Counselling and Psychotherapy Journal, 13,* 20–21.

Gist, R., & Devilly, G. (2002). Post-trauma debriefing: The road too frequently traveled. *Lancet, 360,* 741–743.

Gist, R., & Woodall, S. (1998). Social science versus social movements: The origins and natural history of debriefing. *Australasian Journal of Disaster and Trauma Studies, 2 (1).* Retrieved June 5, 2003, from http://www.massey.ac.nz/~trauma.

Harris, M., Baloglu, M., & Stacks, J. (2002). Mental Health of trauma-exposed firefighters and critical incident stress debriefing. *Journal of Loss and Trauma, 7,* 223–238.

Hiley-Young, B., & Gerrity, E. (1994). Critical incident stress debriefing (CISD): Value and limitations in disaster response. *NCPTSD Clinical Quarterly, 4, (2).* Retrieved May 26, 2003, from http://www.ncptsd.org/publications.

Hollister, R. (1996). Critical incident stress debriefing and the community health nurse. *Journal of Community Health Nursing, 13,* 43–49.

Irving, P., & Long, A. (2001). Critical incident stress debriefing following traumatic life experiences. *Journal of Psychiatric and Mental Health Nursing, 8,* 307–314.

Jambois-Rankin, K. (2000). Critical incident stress debriefing: An examination of public services personnel and their responses to critical incident stress. *Illness, Crisis, & Loss, 8,* 71–90.

Juhnke, G. (1997). After school violence: An adapted critical incident stress debriefing model for student survivors. *Elementary School Guidance and Counseling, 31,* 163–171.

Kroshus, J., & Swarthout, D. (1995). Critical incident stress among funeral directors: Identifying factors relevant for mental health counseling. *Journal of Mental Health Counseling, 17, 4*. Retrieved June 3, 2003, from http://www.web2.epnet.com. June 3, 2003.

LeBrocq, P., Charles, A., Chan, T., & Buchana, M. (2003). Establishing a bereavement program: Caring for the bereaved families and staff in the emergency department. *Accident and Emergency Nursing, 11, 85–90.*

Leonard, R., & Alison, L. (1999). Critical incident stress debriefing and its effects on coping strategies and anger in a sample of Australian police officers involved in shooting incidents. *Work & Stress, 13, 144–161.*

McFarlane, A., & Bookless, C. (2001). The effect of PTSD on interpersonal relationships: Issues for emergency service workers. *Sexual and Relationship Therapy,16, 261–267.*

Moran, C. (1998). Individual differences and debriefing effectiveness. *Australasian Journal of Disaster and Trauma Studies, 1 (2)*. Retrieved June 5, 2003, from http://www.massey.ac.nz/~trauma.

Raphael, B., & Ursano, R. (2002). Psychological debriefing. In Y. Danieli (Ed.), *Sharing the frontline and the back hills: International protectors and providers: Peacekeepers, humanitarians aid workers and the media in the midst of crisis* (pp. 343–352). Amityville, NY: Baywood.

Richards, D. (2001). A field study of critical incident stress debriefing versus critical incident stress management. *Journal of Mental Health, 10, 351–362.*

Sacks, S., Clements, P., & Fay-Hillier, T. (2001). Care after chaos: Use of Critical Incident Stress Debriefing after traumatic workplace events. *Perspectives in Psychiatric Care, 37, 133–136.*

Spitzer, W., & Burke, L. (1993). A critical incident stress debriefing program for hospital-based health care personnel. *Health & Social Work, 18, 149–157.*

Suserud, B., Blomquist, M., & Johansson, I. (2002). Experiences of threats and violence in the Swedish ambulance service. *Accident and Emergency Nursing, 10, 127–135.*

Suserud, B. (2001). How do ambulance personnel experience work at a disaster site? *Accident & Emergency Nursing, 9, 56–66.*

Tobin, J. (2001). The limitations of critical incident stress debriefing. *Irish Journal of Psychiatric Medicine, 18, 142–143.*

Turnbull, G., Busuttil, W., & Pittman, S. (1997). Psychological debriefing for victims of acute burn trauma. *British Journal of Psychiatry, 171, 582.*

van Emmerik, A., Kamphuis, J., Hulsbosch, A., & Emmelkamp, P. (2002). Single session debriefing after psychological trauma: A meta-analysis. *Lancet, 360, 766–771.*

Van Patten, I., & Burke, T. (2001). Critical incident stress and the child homicide investigator. *Homicide Studies, 5, 131–152.*

CHAPTER 7 VICARIOUS TRAUMATIZATION

Black, S., & Weinreich, P. (2001). An exploration of counselling identity in counsellors who deal with trauma. *Traumatology 6, (3)*. Retrieved May 19, 2003, from http://www.fsu.edu/~trauma.

Blair, D., & Ramones, V. (1996). Understanding vicarious traumatization. *Journal of Psychosocial Nursing, 34, 24–30.*

Brady, J., Guy, J., Poelstra, P., & Brokaw, B. (1999). Vicarious traumatization, spirituality, and the treatment of sexual abuse survivors. A national survey of women psychotherapists. *Professional Psychology: Research and Practice, 30, 386–393.*

Crothers, D. (1995). Vicarious traumatization in the work with survivors of childhood trauma. *Journal of Psychosocial Nursing and Mental Health Services, 33, 9–13.*

Dane, B., & Chachkes, E. (2001). The cost of caring for patients with an illness: Contagion to the social worker. *Social Work in Health Care, 33,* 31–51.

Etherington, K. (2000). Supervising counselors who work with survivors of childhood sexual abuse. *Counseling Psychology Quarterly, 13,* 377–390.

Everly, G., Boyle, S., & Lating, J. (1999). The effectiveness of psychological debriefing with vicarious trauma: A meta-analysis. *Stress Medicine, 15,* 229–233.

Goldenberg, J. (2002). The impact on the interviewer of holocaust survivor narratives: Vicarious traumatization or transformation? *Traumatology, 8,* 215–231.

Horwitz, M. (1998). Social worker trauma: Building resilience in child protection social workers. *Smith College Studies in Social Work, 68,* 363–377.

Iliffe, G., & Steed, L. (2000). Exploring the counselor's experience of working with perpetrators and survivors of domestic violence. *Journal of Interpersonal Violence, 15,* 393–412.

Johnson, C., & Hunter, M. (1997). Vicarious traumatization in counsellors working in the New Wales Sexual Assault Service: An exploratory study. *Work & Stress, 11,* 319–328.

Little, S. (2002). Vicarious traumatisation. *Emergency Nurse, 10,* 27–30.

McCann, L., & Pearlman, L. (1990). *Psychological trauma and the adult survivor.* New York: Brunner/Mazel.

Miller, D. (1992, September). Care for the caregivers. *Registered Nurse,* 58–60.

Neumann, D., & Gamble, S. (1995). Issues in the professional development of psychotherapists: Countertransference and vicarious traumatization in the new trauma therapist. *Psychotherapy, 32,* 341–347.

Pearlman, L., & MacIan, P. (1995). Vicarious traumatization: An empirical study of the effects of trauma work on trauma therapists. *Professional Psychology: Research and Practice, 26,* 558–565.

Pearlman, L., & Saakvitne, K. (1995). *Trauma and the therapist: Countertransference and vicarious traumatization in psychotherapy with incest survivors.* New York: Norton.

Pines, A., & Aronson, E. (1988). *Career burnout: Causes and cures* (2nd ed.). New York: Free Press.

Ruzek, J. (1993). Professionals coping with vicarious traumatization. *NCPTSD Clinical Newsletter, 3,* (2). Retrieved May 26, 2003, from http://www.ncptsd.org./publications/cq/v3/n2/ruzek.html.

Saakvitne, K. (1995). Therapists' responses to dissociative clients: Countertransference and vicarious traumatization. In L. Cohen, J. Berzoff, & M. Elin (Eds.), *Dissociative identity disorder: Theoretical and treatment controversies* (pp. 467–492). Northvale, NJ: Aronson.

Saakvitne, K., & Pearlman, L. (1996). *Transforming the pain: A workbook on vicarious traumatization for helping professionals who work with traumatized clients.* New York: Norton.

Sabin-Farrell, R., & Turpin, G. (2003). Vicarious traumatization: Implications for the mental health of health workers? *Clinical Psychology Review, 23,* 449–480.

Schauben, L., & Frazier, P. (1995). Vicarious trauma: The effects on female counselors working with sexual violence survivors. *Psychology of Women Quarterly, 19,* 49–54.

Sexton, L. (1999). Vicarious traumatisation of counsellors and effects on their workplaces. *British Journal of Guidance and Counselling, 27,* 393–404.

Steed, L., & Downing, R. (1998). A phenomenological study of vicarious traumatisation among psychologists and professional counsellors working in the field of sexual abuse/assault. *Australasian Journal of Disaster and Trauma Studies, 2 (3).* Retrieved June 5, 2003, from http://www.massey.ac.nz/~trauma.

CHAPTER 8 BURNOUT

Ackerly, G., Burnell, J., Holder, D., & Kurdek, L. (1988). Burnout among licensed psychologists. *Professional Psychology: Research and Practice, 19,* 624–631.

Aiken, L., Clarke, S., Sloane, D., Sochalski, J., & Silber, J. (2002). Hospital nurse staffing and patient mortality, nurse burnout, and job dissatisfaction. *Journal of the American Medical Association, 288,* 1987–1995.

Alexander, M., & Hegarty, J. (2000). Measuring staff burnout in a community home. *British Journal of Developmental Disabilities, 46,* 51–62.

Balevre P. (2001). Professional nursing burnout and irrational thinking. *Journal of Nurses Staff Development, 17,* 264–271.

Buunk, B., Ybema, J., Van Der Zee, K., Schaufeli, W., & Gibbons, F. (2001). Affect generated by social comparisons among nurses high and low in burnout. *Journal of Applied Social Psychology, 31,* 1500–1521.

Carrilio, T., & Eisenberg, D. (1984). Using peer support to prevent worker burnout. *Social Casework, 65,* 307–310.

Clarkson, P. (1992). Burnout: Typical racket systems of professional helpers. *Transactional Analysis Journal, 22,* 153–158.

Cocco, E., Gatti, M., Lima, C., & Camus, V. (2002). A comparative study of stress and burnout among staff caregivers in nursing homes and acute geriatric wards. *International Journal of Geriatric Psychiatry, 18,* 78–85.

Evans, T., & Villavisanis, R. (1997). Encouragement exchange: Avoiding therapist burnout. *The Family Journal, 5,* 342–345.

Farber, B. (Ed.). (1983). *Stress and burnout in the human service professions.* New York: Pergamon Press.

Figley, C. (Ed.). (1995). *Compassion fatigue: Coping with secondary traumatic stress disorder in those who treat the traumatized.* New York: Brunner/Mazel.

Freudenberger, H. (1974). Staff burnout. *Journal of Social Issues, 30,* 159–165.

Gabassi, P., Cervai, S., Rozbowsky, P., Semeraro, A., & Gregori, D. (2002). Burnout syndrome in the helping professions. *Psychological Reports, 90,* 309–314.

Garrett, D., & McDaniel, A. (2001). A new look at nurse burnout: The effects of environmental uncertainty and social climate. *Journal of Nursing Administration, 31,* 91–96.

Goldberger, L., and Breznitz, S. (Eds.). (1993). *Handbook of stress: Theoretical and clinical aspects* (2nd ed.). New York: Free Press.

Graham, J., Potts, W., & Ramirez, A. (2002). Stress and burnout in doctors. *Lancet, 360,* 1975–1976.

Grosch, W., & Olsen, D. (1994). *When helping starts to hurt: A new look at burnout among psychotherapists.* New York: Norton.

Gundersen, L. (2001). Physician burnout. *Annals of Internal Medicine, 135,* 145–149.

Happell, B., Martin, T., & Pinikahana, J. (2003). Burnout and job satisfaction: A comparative study of psychiatric nurses from forensic and a mainstream mental health service. *International Journal of Mental Health Nursing, 12,* 39–47.

Hawkins, H. (2001). Police officer burnout: A partial replication of Maslach's Burnout Inventory. *Police Quarterly, 4,* 343–360.

Hope, J. (2000). Physician, heal thyself. *Modern Physician, 4,* 88–91.

Huebner, S. (1993). Professionals under stress: A review of burnout among the helping professions with implications for school psychologists. *Psychology in the Schools, 30,* 40–49.

Kluger, M., Townend, K., & Laidlaw, T. (2003). *Job satisfaction, stress and burnout in Australian specialist anaesthetists. Anaesthesia, 58,* 339–345.

Koeske, G., & Kelly, T. (1995). The impact of overinvolvement on burnout and job satisfaction. *American Journal of Orthopsychiatry, 65,* 282–292.

Korkeila, J., Toyry, S., Kumpulainen, K., Toivola, J., Rasanen, K., & Kalimo, R. (2003). Burnout and self-perceived health among Finnish psychiatrists and child psychiatrists: A national survey. *Scandinavian Journal of Public Health, 31,* 85–91.

Leiter, M., Harvie, P., & Frizzell, C. (1998). The correspondence of patient satisfaction and nurse burnout. *Social Science & Medicine, 47,* 1611–1618.

Linehan, M., Cochran, B., Mar, C., Levensky, E., & Comtois, K. (2000). Therapeutic burnout among borderline personality disordered clients and their therapists: Development and evaluation of two adaptations of the Maslach Burnout Inventory. *Cognitive and Behavioral Practice, 7*, 329–337.

Maslach, C. (1982). *Burnout: The cost of caring*. Upper Saddle River, NJ: Prentice Hall.

McCarthy, W., & Frieze, I. (1999). Negative aspects of therapy: Client perceptions of therapists' social influence, burnout, and quality of care. *Journal of Social Issues, 55*, 33–50.

Morgan, R., Van Haveren, R., & Pearson, C. (2002). Correctional officer burnout: Further Analysis. *Criminal Justice and Behavior, 29*, 144–160.

Ospina-Kammerer, V., & Figley, C. (2003). An evaluation of the Respiratory One method (ROM) in reducing emotional exhaustion among family physician residents. *International Journal of Emergency Mental Health, 5*, 29–32.

Pines, A., & Aronson, E. (1988). *Career burnout: Causes and cures* (2nd ed.). New York: Free Press.

Pines, A. (1993). Burnout. In L. Goldberger and S. Breznitz (Eds.), *Handbook of Stress: Theoretical and Clinical Aspects* (2nd Ed.). New York: Free Press.

Potter, B. (1983). Job burnout and the helping professional. *Clinical Gerontologist, 2* 63–65.

Poulin, J., & Walker, C. (1993). Social worker burnout: A longitudinal study. *Social Work Research & Abstracts, 29*, 5–12.

Proctor, B., & Steadman, T. (2003). Job satisfaction, burnout, and perceived effectiveness of "in-house" versus traditional school psychologists. *Psychology in the Schools, 40*, 237–243.

Shapiro, J., Dorman, R., Burkey, W., & Welker, C. (1999). Predictors of job satisfaction and burnout in child abuse professionals: Coping, cognition, and victimization history. *Journal of Child Sexual Abuse, 7*, 23–42.

Shoptaw, S., Stein, J., & Rawson, R. (2000). Burnout in substance abuse counselors: Impact of environment, attitudes, and clients with HIV. *Journal of Substance Abuse Treatment, 19*, 117–126.

Sims, K. (2001). Hardiness & spiritual well-being: Moderators of professional nurse burnout. Mapping the Journey for Research and Practice. *Community Nurse Research, 34*, 247.

Skovholt, T., Grier, T., & Hanson, M. (2001). Career counseling for longevity: Self-care and burnout prevention strategies for counselor resilience. *Journal of Career Development, 27*, 167–176.

Soderfeldt, M., Soderfeldt, B., & Warg, L. (1995). Burnout in social work. *Social Work, 40*, 638–646.

Spickard, A., Gabbe, S., & Christensen, J. (2002). Mid-career burnout in generalists and specialist physicians. *Journal of the American Medical Association, 288*, 1447–1450.

Stevens, M., & Higgins, D. (2002). The influence of risk and protective factors on burnout experienced by those who work with maltreated children. *Child Abuse Review, 11*, 313–331.

Thorpe, G., Righthand, S., & Kubik, E. (2001). Brief report: Dimensions of burnout in professionals working with sex offenders. *Sexual Abuse: Journal of Research & Treatment, 13*, 197–203.

Tilley, S., & Chambers, M. (2003). The effectiveness of clinical supervision on burnout amongst community mental health nurses in Wales. *Journal of Psychiatric and Mental Health Nursing, 10*, 231–238.

Um, M., & Harrison, D. (1998). Role stressors, burnout, mediators, and job satisfaction: A stress-strain-outcome model and an empirical test. *Social Work Research, 22*, 100–116.

Violanti, J. (2001). Posttraumatic stress disorder intervention in law enforcement: Differing perspectives. *Australasian Journal of Disaster and Trauma Studies, 2 (6)*. Retrieved June 5, 2003, from http://www.massey.ac.nz/~trauma.

Williams, C. (1989). Empathy and burnout in male and female helping professionals. *Research in Nursing and Health, 12,* 169–178.

Zaslove, M. (2001). A case of physician burnout. *American Family Physician, 64,* 517–519.

Index

Author Biography

Patrick J. Morrissette. Ph.D., RMFT, CCC, NCC, is a Full Professor of Health Studies at Brandon University, Manitoba, Canada. He holds a joint appointment in the First Nations and Aboriginal Counselling program and the Bachelor of Science in Psychiatric Nursing program. He completed his master's degree in Counseling at Niagara University (New York) and his doctoral studies in Counselling Psychology at the University of Alberta. In addition to being a Clinical Member and Approved Supervisor with the American Association for Marriage and Family Therapy, Patrick is a Registered Marriage and Family Therapist in Canada, Certified Canadian Counsellor, and a Certified Counselor with National Board of Certified Counselors.

Dr. Morrissette is cofounder of *Peaceful Futures*, a couples therapy program sponsored by Family Violence Prevention Program, Province of Manitoba Family Services and Housing. For the past 26 years, Patrick has worked, supervised, and consulted in a variety of inpatient and outpatient treatment centers in both Canada and the United States.

Patrick's scholarly and research contributions to the counseling profession have resulted in national awards. To date he has published 60 articles and contributed chapters and is the author of *Self-Supervision: A Primer for Counselors and Helping Professionals* (2001, Brunner-Routledge) and coauthor of *Effective Interviewing of Children: A Comprehensive Guide for Counselors and Human Service Workers* (1999, Accelerated Development).